CONTENTS

A Practical Guide to
Working with Parents
2nd Edition

Christine Hobart
Jill Frankel

Series Editor: Miranda Walker

OXFORD
UNIVERSITY PRESS

OXFORD

UNIVERSITY PRESS

Great Clarendon Street, Oxford, OX2 6DP, United Kingdom

Oxford University Press is a department of the University of Oxford.
It furthers the University's objective of excellence in research, scholarship,
and education by publishing worldwide. Oxford is a registered trade mark of
Oxford University Press in the UK and in certain other countries

Text © Christine Hobart and Jill Frankel 2003
Original illustrations © Oxford University Press 2014

First published by Nelson Thornes Ltd in 2003
This edition published by Oxford University Press in 2014

British Library Cataloguing in Publication Data
Data available

978-1-4085-0480-2

2

Printed in Great Britain

Acknowledgements

Illustrations: Jane Bottomley and Ian Heard
Page make-up: Northern Phototypesetting
Picture research: Sue Sharp

Although we have made every effort to trace and contact all
copyright holders before publication this has not been possible in all
cases. If notified, the publisher will rectify any errors or omissions at
the earliest opportunity.

ABOUT THE AUTHORS

Christine Hobart and Jill Frankel come from a background of health visiting and nursery education. They worked together in Camden before meeting again at City and Islington College. They have worked together for many years, training students to work with young children and have written twelve books encompassing all areas of the childcare curriculum. Christine is an external examiner for CACHE.

Miranda Walker has worked with children from birth to 16 years in a range of settings, including her own day nursery and out of school clubs. She has inspected nursery provision for Ofsted, and worked at East Devon College as an Early Years and Playwork lecturer and NVQ assessor and internal verifier. She is a regular contributor to industry magazines and an established author.

DEDICATION

For our mothers

ACKNOWLEDGEMENTS

The authors and publishers would like to thank the following people and organisations for permission to use material:

- Bowes Primary School for permission to use the Home/School Agreement on pages 79–80, The Family Liaison Work Statement on page 120 and the Complaints Process on page 158.
- Friends of Bowes, for the agenda on page 71.
- Hampden Way Nursery School for 'Parents and the Nursery' on page 51, Settling-in Policy on pages 56–60 and extracts from the Nursery School Brochure on pages 72–5.
- Lorna, Victoria and Theo at Hampden Way Nursery School for the Home–School Diary on page 77.
- Marian Beaver, *Babies and Young Children: Diploma in Child Care and Education* for the text on pages 156–7.

In addition, we would like to thank the following for permission to use photographs:

The Kelly family page 30, Marian Beaver page 31, The National Portrait Gallery, London page 2, Peter M. Fisher/Corbis page 36, Photodisc 45 (NT) page 40, Photodisc 66 (NT) page 104, Photodisc 73 (NT) page 7, Photofusion pages 110 and 148.

Every attempt has been made to contact copyright holders and we apologise if any have been overlooked. Should copyright have been unwittingly infringed in this book, the owners should contact the publishers, who will make corrections at reprint.

INTRODUCTION

In the experience of the authors, there are no basic guides offering help to child-care and education students working with the parents of young children. New students often enrol on courses to work with children without appreciating how much contact they will have with children's families and not realising how much they will be assessed on the way they communicate and work in partnership with the parents.

In our view, the more knowledge and information that students can obtain, the better they will understand the role of parents in their children's education and development. A greater understanding of a wide range of various family structures, parenting styles and child rearing practices will enable students to develop good practice and allow them to support parents in times of stress. It is often difficult for placement supervisors to permit students to have much contact with parents because of the rules of confidentiality, lack of experience and the short time the student might spend in the placement, so we trust this book will make it easier for students to make a valuable contribution.

The book is designed to be user-friendly. Most chapters contain the following features:

- Charts
- Case studies
- Good practice
- Activities
- Resources such as organisations, websites and helplines.

We have used the female gender for the child in every chapter as this is less confusing than continually changing gender.

1 PARENTS TODAY

For children to develop successfully and reach their full potential, a strong positive relationship between parents, teachers and professional caregivers is essential. You need to have a good understanding of how all families function in our society, and how you can contribute constructively as a child-care and education practitioner.

Sharing the care and education of children with their parents is a privilege and a professional responsibility. To do this to the best of your ability you will need knowledge, and communication and practical skills. Bringing up children today is very different from 100 years ago and ideas of parenting are always subject to change, depending on the prevailing trends in the society. During the last 30 years, women and ethnic groups have gradually attained more rights and more control over their lives. At the beginning of this century the birthrate has dropped to less than two children per family and the divorce rate is approaching 40%. Couples are redefining their relationships, with many rejecting the notion of marriage.

In this time of rapid change, some parents find their role confusing. Children are more exposed to forces outside the family, such as television, the Internet and pressure from peers. Many parents find it hard to provide love and security while still setting clear boundaries for acceptable behaviour. There has been a loss of confidence in the role of those in authority, following scandals in such diverse groups as the police, judges and the clergy. Children are becoming better informed about their rights through discussion, school councils and access to the media.

Developing a partnership

Since the beginning of the 20th century educationalists have realised the value of involving parents in the education of their children. As early as 1905 teachers were given an official handbook to encourage them to influence parents. Rachel and Margaret McMillan were convinced that nursery education must include the education and involvement of the parents as well as the children. They encouraged Open Days when parents could watch the activities in the nursery.

Activity
Find out what you can about Rachel and Margaret McMillan. Why were they so influential as educators?

Margaret McMillan

The Hadow Report (1931) stated that Parent Associations should be set up and that medical inspections should be carried out with the parents present. Teachers were to dispense advice to 'ignorant but grateful' parents.

In 1947 Cyril Burt, looking at the relationship between home background and attainment in *The Backward Child*, found the most important variable to be parents' aspirations for their children's achievement.

In 1961 the Pre-school Playgroups Association was established. Local parents set up and ran nursery education groups for their own children as the government was reluctant to spend money on early years provision.

In 1967, the Plowden Report on primary schools devoted a whole chapter to parent participation and made the following recommendations:

- All schools should have a programme for contact with children's homes to include meeting the parents before the child starts school. There should also be formal private talks, open days, school booklets and written reports, and information about the child's work should be shared with the parents. Schools should make an effort to meet parents who did not visit the school.
- The education department should issue a booklet containing examples of good practice in parent–teacher relations.
- Parents should be allowed to choose their children's primary school whenever possible.
- Primary schools should be used as much as possible out of school hours, with the heads having a say in the use of the buildings.
- Parents should be invited to help with out-of-school activities.
- Community schools should be developed in all areas.

After this report, there was a certain amount of involvement but no suggestion of mutual responsibility or of parents being involved in the management or organisation of their children's schools. It was also explicitly stated that full-time nursery education should not be provided to allow women to work.

In 1972 a White Paper, *Framework for Expansion*, promised nursery provision for all families that wanted it. Some of the research that followed looked at the part parents could play in the schools. The Thomas Coram Research Unit looked into parents reading with their children at home. The researchers, Jack Tizard and Jenny Hewison, discovered that, with careful explanations and monitoring by teachers, parents were willing and able to participate and the reading age in the schools that took part went up considerably in contrast to control schools. Barbara Tizard was then funded to carry out action research in parental involvement in seven pre-school groups. The Oxford pre-school research group, headed by J.S. Bruner, looked into various pre-schools. One conclusion was the need for greater involvement of parents.

All research in the 1970s and 80s seemed to indicate not only evidence of a great desire among parents of all classes to help with their children's education but also that they were extremely good at doing so if the staff in the schools only took the time and trouble to explain what they wanted the parents to do. Today's parents are encouraged to read to their pre-school children and also to their babies almost from birth.

The Taylor report (1977) recommended that two parents should be on each school's governing body. It also suggested that the governing body should satisfy itself that adequate arrangements were made to inform parents, to involve them in their children's progress and welfare, to enlist their support and to ensure that they had access to the school and teachers by reasonable arrangement.

Bruner in 1980 noted that 'One needs to ensure that parents keep confidence in their own skills as child-rearers. They must be encouraged to feel that they too can have a large and expert hand in raising their children'. It is important for early years workers to remember this, as if parents feel de-skilled their lack of self-esteem may be reflected in the children.

In 1996, the School Curriculum and Assessment Authority produced some guidelines for establishments to work more closely with parents. Partnership should be based on:

- shared responsibility
- understanding and mutual respect
- development of communication and dialogue.

Margy Whalley at the Pen Green Centre has stated that 'a real partnership with parents involves power sharing, a recognition of parents' equally valuable knowledge and expertise, and an understanding of the real pressures that young families face. Projects that aim to do things to parents are generally much less effective than projects where parents are intrinsically motivated – where they are doing things for themselves.'

Today, partnership with parents should mean true partnership, with schools, parents and nurseries working together with establishments and parents feeling that they are making an equal contribution to the care and education of the child. The aim is to move on from 'involvement', where the power was with the establishment.

Recent trends in parenting

The homes and lives of children in the UK have changed dramatically in the last 30 years. There are many possible reasons for this:

- increase in divorce and the number of households headed by one parent
- increase in mobility, so that young families do not always have the support of an extended family
- increase in the number of step families, and in the number of different relationships that the parents might have
- increase in stress, due to uncertainty in employment or longer hours in the workplace
- increase in the number of children living in relative poverty
- increase in drug and alcohol abuse
- increase in violence on television, film and video
- increase in reporting of violence in the media, which has led to fear of allowing children to be independent outside the home
- increase in house-husbands/partners
- increase in the involvement of the father in some aspects of child rearing
- increase in the number of much smaller families so that fewer children grow up with the opportunity to learn about the care of babies and children through direct observation.

In some ways, the home has become a more claustrophobic place. Many children do not have so much freedom to play outside and spend more time in front of computers, televisions and videos. The 2001 census of England and Wales found that 702,000 children lived in flats above the ground floor and 40,000 on the fifth floor or higher. Opportunities for outside play were restricted for the 8.9% of children under 3 living above the ground floor.

In the UK families can now choose when to have their children, how many to have, how the money is earned, who stays home with the children and what child-care to choose. At the time of writing:

- women are entitled to 52 weeks maternity leave. If eligible for statutory maternity pay, they are entitled to 39 weeks of pay at £123.06 per week
- men are entitled to two weeks paid paternity leave within 8 weeks of the birth
- rights for parents of children under 6 and disabled children up to the age of 18 to request working flexible hours – employers are obliged to take these requests seriously
- leave for parents adopting a child, when the child is first placed with them.

Activity
There have been many social changes during the last 30 years.
1 How do you think this has affected the lives of the children?
2 What affect have these changes had on the lives of the parents?

A recent report by the National Centre for Research showed that a third of fathers work 10-hour days, the longest hours in Europe, and come home absolutely exhausted. It shows that in most dual-income families one or both parents work outside the standard 9–5 8-hour day. More than half of employed lone mothers also work atypical hours. Couples who work at unusual times tend to operate a shift system of parenting, so that at least one of them is looking after the children at any time.

Some parents are starting their families at a later age. House prices are high, and there is a need to earn more to pay bigger mortgages. Many mothers wish to remain on the career ladder for longer, so most go back to work within 13 months.

A recent survey of 1,100 parents showed that:
- 53% of the mothers said they took responsibility for more of the decisions about the children
- 71% of mothers said they would be more likely to stay at home if the child was sick
- 65% of mothers said they spent more than 15 hours a week alone with their child, compared to 18% of the fathers
- 35% of fathers spent less than 5 hours a week alone with their children.

In England 30% of children are born to unmarried mothers and the UK has the highest rate in Europe of single mothers in their teens.

Becoming a parent

People decide to live together for many reasons, mainly for emotional and financial support. They see becoming parents as a natural extension of the partnership but do not always realise the impact that having children will have on their relationship.

Once a pregnancy is established and has been accepted as a definite event, one or both of the parties may have mixed feelings about the forthcoming birth. There may be all sorts of doubts due to their own upbringing. All this may strain the relationship. The father is expected to support the mother but he may have his own hopes and fears that need to be addressed. This might be difficult for him to do once faced with a *fait accompli*.

During the pregnancy, the couple may have an idealised picture of the future. The reality is often different. It is important for partners to discuss prior to the baby's birth their relationship and how it will be affected. The changes to their lifestyle need to be discussed and priorities agreed. There may be a shift in responsibilities once the baby is born, with the mother expected to take on a more domestic role if she is no longer working. It may also be difficult for the mother not to earn her own money and to have to account for her spending to her partner, resulting in diminished self esteem.

The baby will make exhausting demands on both parents, and the mother in particular if she is breast-feeding. The father may feel that his place in his partner's affections has been usurped by the baby, as the mother is often too tired to give him the time and love he is used to. This often coincides with the father having to work longer hours to replace the income of the mother and to provide for the needs of the baby.

Being a parent does not stop at babyhood, but is for life. It has been suggested that there are six stages of parenthood:

1 Pregnancy: parents imagine their child, anticipate their future and make plans for the baby.
2 Infancy: bonding and attachment takes place, the parents learn to anticipate the needs of the child and come to terms with reality.
3 Pre-schoolers: setting guidelines and boundaries while promoting growing independence; handling challenging behaviour with firmness and understanding.
4 School-aged child: allowing the child autonomy and the freedom to make relationships with peers; assisting the child in her all round development.
5 Adolescence: accepting the child's independence, helping her cope with physical and emotional changes while still insisting on guidelines for behaviour.
6 Leaving home: accepting your child as an adult who is taking responsibility for her own life.

Bavelock (1990) suggested that parents need to develop emotionally and cognitively, as the following diagram shows.

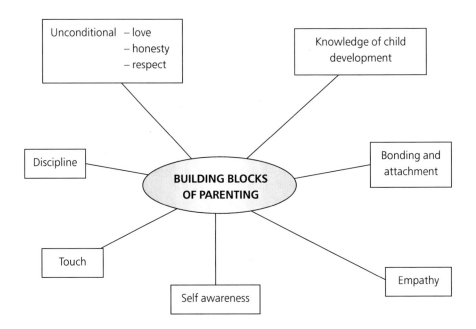

The parental role

The National Children's Bureau, in its book *Confident Parents, Confident Children: policy and practice in parent education and support* (1994), included the following advertisement:

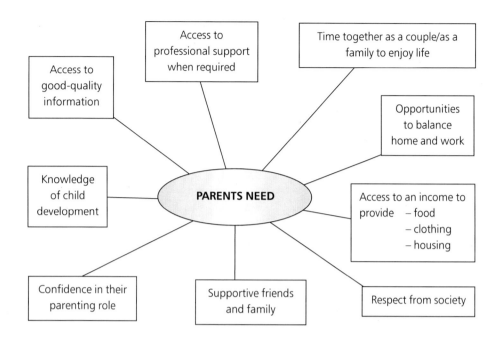

To carry out the parental role satisfactorily parents need to:
- provide an environment where children can be nurtured and fulfil their developmental potential
- have expectations for their children that are realistic yet encourage them to develop their own ideas
- set consistent boundaries for their children's behaviour
- protect their children from danger while allowing them to become independent
- give their children choices, allowing them to make mistakes and understand the consequences of their actions
- listen to their children, remember that children have rights as well as parents and understand their point of view
- have time management and organisational skills to meet the demands of home, school and work
- pass on the values and mores of their heritage and code of behaviour
- help their children to develop a sense of self esteem and individuality
- have supportive family and friends
- have access to information and support services
- have time away from their children occasionally to reflect on their role, refresh themselves and meet their own needs.

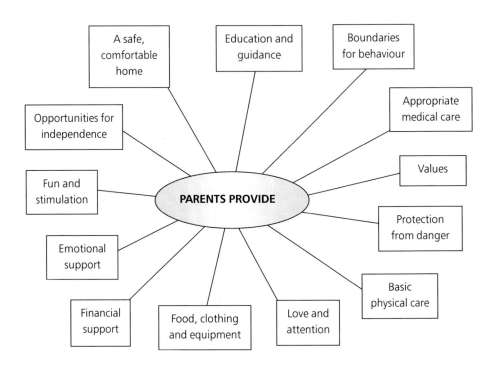

Parenting will be influenced by

■ upbringing, the way the parents themselves were parented
■ economic circumstances, such as income, employment and housing
■ class and education
■ religion and culture
■ the media
■ advances in technology
■ changes in society, political and moral.

It is an extremely demanding job being a parent. It is important to recognise that all parents want the best for their children and that being a parent is a complex role. In general, if it appears that the parents are not always able to meet their children's needs, this is usually due to external forces such as unemployment or bereavement rather than lack of love or thought on their part. Considering the very real sacrifices that parents make in order to do the best for their children, it is amazing how many good parents there are.

It was Donald Winnicott who spoke about 'good enough parents' who do everything they can to provide the emotional and physical conditions for a child to develop satisfactorily to adulthood, given the prevailing imperfections of environment and human frailty. Good enough parents know they are doing their best under the circumstances and are content with what they do.

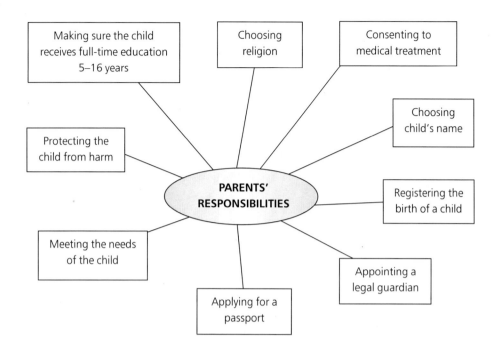

Making sure the child receives full-time education 5–16 years

Choosing religion

Consenting to medical treatment

Choosing child's name

Protecting the child from harm

PARENTS' RESPONSIBILITIES

Registering the birth of a child

Meeting the needs of the child

Applying for a passport

Appointing a legal guardian

Resources

Websites

www.familyandparenting.org

Organisations

Effective Parenting, 117 Corringham Road, London NW11 7DL. Telephone: 0208 458 8404
Exploring Parenthood
National Childbirth Trust, www.nctpregnancyand babycare.com/home
National Children's Bureau, www.ncb.org.uk/Page.asp
Parent Line, www.parentlineplus.org.uk
Pippin (Parents in partnership – parent infant network)

2 *THE LEGAL FRAMEWORK*

This chapter covers:
- **The rights of children**
- **The Children Act 1989**
- **National Childcare Strategy**
- **The Parents' Charter**
- **Early years intervention programmes**

In recent times there has been a great deal of legislation affecting children and their families, and there have been many government initiatives. This has led to early intervention programmes to help children get a good start in life. Anyone working with children and their families needs to be aware of existing legislation to inform good practice and to be a professional source of information for parents.

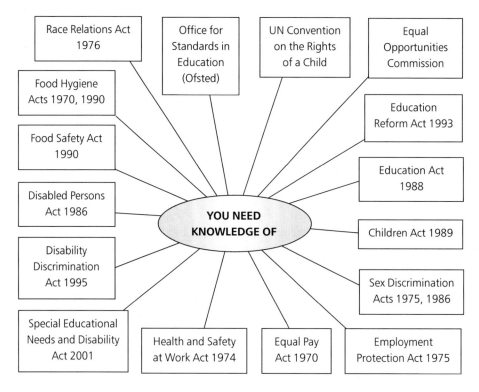

The rights of children

To play an effective part in working with children and their parents it is important for you to have a clear understanding of the UN Convention on the rights of children, the legal framework and the national and local guidelines published for all professionals working with children.

The important points made by the UN Convention are as follows:

- Article 5: Governments should respect the rights and responsibilities of families to direct and guide their children so that, as they grow, they learn to use their rights properly.
- Article 7: All children have the right to a legally registered name and nationality, also the right to know and as far as possible to be cared for by their parents.
- Article 8: Governments should respect children's right to a name, a nationality and family ties.
- Article 9: Children should not be separated from their parents unless it is for their own good – for example, if a parent is mistreating or neglecting a child. Children whose parents have separated have the right to stay in contact with both parents unless this might hurt the child.
- Article 10: Families who live in different countries should be allowed to move between those countries so that parents and children can stay in contact or get back together as a family.
- Article 14: Children have the right to think and believe what they want and to practise their religion as long as they are not stopping other people from enjoying their rights. Parents should guide their children on these matters.
- Article 18: Both parents share responsibility for bringing up their children and should always consider what is best for each child. Governments should help parents by providing services to support them, especially if both parents work.
- Article 19: Governments should ensure that children are properly cared for, and protect them from violence, abuse and neglect by their parents or anyone else who looks after them.
- Article 29: Education should develop each child's personality and talents to the full. It should encourage children to respect their parents, and their own and other cultures.

The Children Act 1989

The Children Act 1989 has had a major impact on the law relating to children, affecting all children and their families. Much of the pre-existing law was abolished. The emphasis of the new law is that parents should have responsibility for their children, rather than rights over them. Parental responsibility is defined as the rights, duties, powers, responsibilities and authority, which by law a parent of a child has in relation to the child and his or her property. The Children Act acknowledges the importance of the wishes of the child. Parental rights diminish as the child matures.

Parental responsibility is a concept that it is important to understand when working out who is in a position to make decisions about the child and who should be contacted in any legal proceedings. Those who can hold parental responsibility are:

- the mother, who always has it, whether married or not – she can only lose it when an adoption or freeing order is made
- the natural father, who has it jointly with the natural mother if they are married to each other at the time of the child's birth or subsequently marry. In these circumstances he too can only lose it if an adoption or freeing order is made
- the natural father, if not married to the mother, may acquire it by agreement with her, or by court order
- a step-parent can acquire it by obtaining a residence order and will lose it if that order ends
- the local authority acquires it when obtaining a care order or emergency protection order and loses it when that order ends
- others, such as grandparents, may acquire it by court order and will lose it when the order ends.

The law has recently changed to extend automatic parental responsibility to the father whose name appears on the child's birth certificate, although, at the time of publication, no implementation date has been set and this date will not be retrospective.

Parental responsibility may not be surrendered or transferred. It can be shared with a number of persons and/or the local authority. Each individual having parental responsibility may act alone in exercising it, but not in a way that is incompatible with any court order made under the Children Act 1989. The Act sets out a series of principles dictating practice and procedure, both in and out of court.

The birth of a child must be registered within 42 days with the Registrar of Births, Marriages and Deaths of the sub-district in which the birth took place.

The key messages of the Children Act 1989 are shown in the chart opposite and on page 18.

THE CHILDREN ACT, 1989

PRINCIPLES OF THE ACT

- Children are generally best looked after within their families.
- Parents and guardians retain parental responsibility and work in partnership with the Local Authority.
- No court order to be made unless better than making no order at all.
- The child's welfare is the court's paramount consideration.
- The Local Authority cannot acquire parental responsibility without a court order.
- Orders available to protect children and avoid unwarranted intervention in family life.

DUTIES AND POWERS

- Identify children in need, safeguard and promote their welfare within their families where consistent.
- Provide a range and level of appropriate services.
- Consult child, parent, those with parental responsibility and others whom the agency considers relevant when making decisions about the child.
- Have regard to child's race, religion, culture and language when making decisions about children being looked after.
- Set up representations and complaints procedure and publish its existence.
- Use orders under Parts IV and V if child is suffering or likely to suffer significant harm.

PRINCIPLES AND PRACTICE GUIDE

- Children, young people and their parents should be considered as individuals with particular needs and potential.
- A child's age, sex, health, personality, race, culture and life experiences are all relevant to any consideration of needs and vulnerability and have to be taken into account when planning or providing help.
- There are unique advantages for children in experiencing normal family life in their own birth family and every effort should be made to preserve the child's home and family links.
- The development of a working partnership with parents is usually the most effective route to providing supplementary or substitute care for their children.
- The wishes of the children should be taken into account. Children should be consulted and kept informed.

▶

- Decisions made in court should be responsive to the needs of children, promote their welfare and reached without undue delay.
- Where children are placed away from home there must be adequate supervision that ensures highest quality substitute parenting with good standards of care and safety.
- Parents; contact with children should be maintained wherever possible.

EQUALITY ISSUES

- Attitudes towards 'The Family' – the influence of institutional, societal and personal belief and experience on assessment and planning.
- Skills and knowledge available to accurately consult with the child, relatives and others.
- Ability to take into account the factors of race, culture, language and religion.
- Ability to understand the effect of disability on the whole family. Parents should be helped to raise the children themselves.
- Openness to working in partnership; developing a combination of anti-discriminatory policies; commitment to guaranteed resource provision; support to enable staff to work with confidence.

In 1990 the National Children's Bureau set out its policy for young children, in particular the under-5s. The principles of this policy are
- that young children are important in their own right and as a resource for the future
- that young children are valued and their full development is possible only if they live in an environment that reflects and respects their individual identity, culture and heritage
- that parents are primarily responsible for nurturing and supporting the development of their children and that this important role should be more highly valued in society
- that central and local government have a duty working in partnership with parents to ensure that services and support are available for families: services that encourage children's cognitive, social, emotional and physical development and meet parents' need for support for themselves and for day care for their children
- that services for young children should be provided within a consistent legal framework that allows for flexibility but ensures basic protection against pain and abuse, equal opportunities and the absence of discrimination, and development of the child as an individual through good quality childcare practice.

National Childcare Strategy

The National Childcare Strategy initiative was set up by the government in 1998. Its main aims were to provide quality, accessible and affordable childcare for under-5s and to provide school children with appropriate childcare and enjoyable activities out of school hours, thus allowing parents to work or train for a career.

Early Years Development and Childcare Partnerships (EYDCPs) were established in all education authorities in England and Wales to deliver the strategy, which entailed drawing up plans to develop local services and to meet targets set by the government. Members of the partnership include representatives from the local authorities, employers, childcare and education providers, parents and other interested organisations. The aims of the National Childcare Strategy are shown on the diagram below:

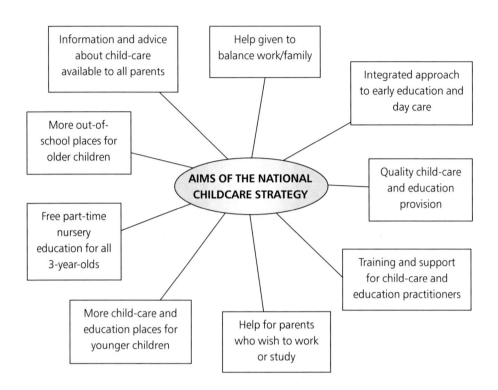

Information and advice about child-care available to all parents	Help given to balance work/family	Integrated approach to early education and day care
More out-of-school places for older children	**AIMS OF THE NATIONAL CHILDCARE STRATEGY**	Quality child-care and education provision
Free part-time nursery education for all 3-year-olds		Training and support for child-care and education practitioners
More child-care and education places for younger children	Help for parents who wish to work or study	

TEN YEAR CHILDCARE STRATEGY

Building on the National Childcare Strategy, in 2004 the Government published the *Ten Year Childcare Strategy: Choice for parents, the best start for children*. Its key themes are:

- *Choice and Flexibility* – greater choice for parents in how they balance their work commitments and family life through enhanced parental leave and easy access to Sure Start children's centres for all (not just families who experience social disadvantage. See pg 23).
- *Availability* – flexible childcare for all families with children aged up to 14 who need it; and 15 hours a week free early education for all 3- and 4-year-olds for 38 weeks a year, with 20 hours as a goal.
- *Quality* – high quality provision delivered by a skilled early years and childcare workforce, with full daycare settings professionally led and a strengthened qualification and career structure.
- *Affordability* – affordable provision appropriate to their needs with substantial increases in tax credit support.

THE CHILDCARE ACT 2006

This Act takes forward some of the key commitments of the Ten Year Childcare Strategy. It introduces the Early Years Foundation Stage (see below) and aims to support settings in providing high quality, integrated care and education for all children aged 0–5 years. It gives local authorities the responsibility to improve outcomes for **all** children under five. Since April 2008, local authorities have also had a duty to provide information, advice and assistance to parents and prospective parents of children and young people up to age 20. You can read more about this on the Every Child Matters website (see the Resources section on page 28).

THE EARLY YEARS FOUNDATION STAGE

Since September 2008, *The Early Years Foundation Stage* (EYFS) has been mandatory for:
■ all schools
■ all early years providers in Ofsted registered settings (including nurseries, pre-schools and childminders).
It applies to children from birth to the end of the academic year in which the child has their fifth birthday.

In the *Statutory Framework for the Early Years Foundation Stage* the Department for Education and Skills tells us that:

'Every child deserves the best possible start in life and support to fulfil their potential. A child's experience in the early years has a major impact on their future life chances. A secure, safe and happy childhood is important in its own right, and it provides the foundation for children to make the most of their abilities and talents as they grow up. When parents choose to use early years services they want to know that provision will keep their children safe and help them to thrive. The Early Years Foundation Stage (EYFS) is the framework that provides that assurance. The overarching aim of the EYFS is to help young children achieve the five *Every Child Matters* outcomes ...'

Every Child Matters is the government agenda which focuses on bringing together services to support children and families. It sets out five major outcomes for children:

- being healthy
- staying safe
- enjoying and achieving
- making a positive contribution
- economic well-being.

The EYFS aims to meet the *Every Child Matters* outcomes by:

- **setting standards** for the learning, development and care young children should experience when they attend a setting outside their family home. Every child should make progress, with no children left behind
- **providing equality of opportunity and anti-discriminatory practice.** Ensuring that every child is included and not disadvantaged because of ethnicity, culture, religion, home language, family background, learning difficulties or disabilities, gender or ability
- **creating a framework for partnership working between parents and professionals**, and between all the settings that the child attends
- **improving quality and consistency in the early years** through standards that apply to all settings. This provides the basis for the inspection and regulation regime carried out by Ofsted
- **laying a secure foundation for future learning** through learning and development that is planned around the individual needs and interests of the child. This is informed by the use of on-going observational assessment.

Note: The EYFS replaces *The Curriculum Guidance for the Foundation Stage, the Birth to Three Matters Framework* and *The National Standards for Under 8s Daycare and Childminding*, which are now defunct. All settings following the EYFS must have regard to the Special Educational Needs Code of Practice 2002.

THE EARLY YEARS FOUNDATION STAGE WELFARE REQUIREMENTS

Settings to which the EYFS applies must also meet the Early Years Foundation Stage welfare requirements. These fall into the following five categories:

Safeguarding and promoting children's welfare

- The provider must take necessary steps to safeguard and promote the welfare of children.
- The provider must promote the good health of the children, take necessary steps to prevent the spread of infection, and take appropriate action when they are ill.

- Children's behaviour must be managed effectively and in a manner appropriate for their stage of development and particular individual needs.

Suitable people
- Providers must ensure that adults looking after children, or having unsupervised access to them, are suitable to do so.
- Adults looking after children must have appropriate qualifications, training, skills and knowledge.
- Staffing arrangements must be organised to ensure safety and to meet the needs of the children.

Suitable premises, environment and equipment
- Outdoor and indoor spaces, furniture, equipment and toys must be safe and suitable for their purpose.

Organisation
- Providers must plan and organise their systems to ensure that every child receives an enjoyable and challenging learning and development experience that is tailored to meet their individual needs.

Documentation
- Providers must maintain records, policies and procedures required for the safe and efficient management of the settings and to meet the needs of the children.

THE CHILDREN'S PLAN

In 2007, the Government published the *Children's Plan* which sets out ambitious new goals for 2020. The Plan is intended to:
- strengthen support for all families during the formative early years of their children's lives
- take the next steps in achieving world class schools and an excellent education for every child
- involve parents fully in their children's learning
- help to make sure that young people have interesting and exciting things to do outside of school
- provide more places for children to play safely.

There will be regular reports on the progress the Government is making. For more information, visit www.dfes.gov.uk/publications/childrensplan/.

SURE START

Sure Start is the Government's programme to deliver the best start in life for every child by bringing together early education, childcare, health and family support. Some Sure Start initiatives apply universally, while others only apply in targeted local areas and/or to disadvantaged groups in England.

Responsibility for Sure Start lies with The Early Years, Extended Schools and Special Needs Group, which belongs to the Department for Children, Schools and Families. Sure Start tells us the following about their service:

Services

- Sure Start covers children from conception through to age 14, and up to age 16 for those with special educational needs and disabilities. It also aims to help parents and communities across the country.
- There are a wide range of services currently available, from Children's Centres and early support programmes to information and advice on health and financial matters. We are helping set and maintain childcare standards.
- Sure Start is the cornerstone of the Government's drive to tackle child poverty and social exclusion working with parents-to-be, parents/carers and children to promote the physical, intellectual and social development of babies and young children so that they can flourish at home and when they get to school.
- All Sure Start local programmes have become children's centres. Local authorities are responsible for Sure Start children's centres, and the services on offer may vary from area to area.

How do our services work?

Our services bring together universal, free, early education and more and better childcare. Sure Start does this with greater support where there is greater need through children's tax credit, children's centres and Sure Start local programmes.

Integrated Early Years Services

For some time we have been encouraging the delivery of childcare alongside early education and other health and family services.

Sure Start Children's Centres

Sure Start Children's Centres are building on existing successful initiatives like Sure Start Local Programmes, Neighbourhood Nurseries and Early Excellence Centres, and bringing high-quality integrated early years services to the heart of communities.

Our target of 2,500 children's centres was reached in early March 2008, and 2,914 centres have now been established (October 2008), offering services to over 2.3 million young children and their families. By 2010, the number of children's centres will increase to 3,500 – so every family has easy access to high-quality integrated services in their community and the benefits of Sure Start can be felt nationwide.

Early Education

All 3- and 4-year-olds are now guaranteed a free, part-time ($12\frac{1}{2}$ hours per week, 38 weeks per year, increasing to 15 hours per week in 2010), early-education place. There are over 37,000 settings delivering free, Government-funded, early education in the maintained, private, voluntary and independent sectors.

Childcare

In June 2008, the stock of registered childcare stood at approaching 1.3 million places (more than double the 1997 level).

There will be a childcare place for all children aged between 3 and 14, between the hours of 8am and 6pm each weekday by 2010, when there will be over 2 million sustainable childcare places for children up to 14.

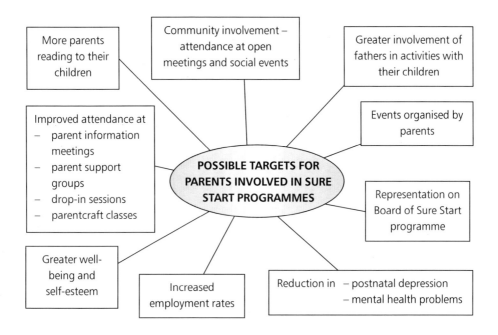

More parents reading to their children

Community involvement – attendance at open meetings and social events

Greater involvement of fathers in activities with their children

Improved attendance at
– parent information meetings
– parent support groups
– drop-in sessions
– parentcraft classes

Events organised by parents

POSSIBLE TARGETS FOR PARENTS INVOLVED IN SURE START PROGRAMMES

Representation on Board of Sure Start programme

Greater well-being and self-esteem

Increased employment rates

Reduction in – postnatal depression
– mental health problems

The Parents' Charter

The Parents' Charter protects the rights of parents to high-quality education for their children. It gives parents the right to demand certain standards and services from schools.

Parents have the right to:

- say what school they want their child to attend and appeal if they do not get their first choice
- see basic performance information on schools
- get a summary of the most recent inspection of their child's school
- get a full written report concerning their child's progress at least once a year.

1 Make sure you understand new legislation and government initiatives.
2 Keep policies and procedures up to date.
3 Be able to explain to parents any changes in family law.
4 Be aware of the stresses on the family today, in maintaining a balance between home and work.
5 Support all parents in their parenting role.
6 Be aware of any local initiatives and participate where possible.

Early years intervention programmes

The growing interest in the involvement of parents in their children's education has inspired a number of intervention programmes targeted at socially disadvantaged families. One of the first, Head Start in the USA, clearly showed that working with families and giving enriched nursery programmes to very young children produced an increase in IQ initially and that, over 20 years, the children were still more socially well adapted and less liable to become delinquent than their control group. Head Start was cost effective in that every £1 spent saved the state £7 later. More students went to college and owned their own homes, and fewer became unemployed, drew benefit, or committed crimes.

HOME START

Programmes were started in the UK in the 1970s. Home Start was one of the first, initiated in Leicester in 1973 and still carrying on today. Home Start is a voluntary organisation, in which volunteers offer regular support, friendship and practical help to young families under stress in their own homes, helping to prevent family crisis and breakdown. The only criterion required to work as a volunteer was to have had your own children.

EDUCATIONAL HOME VISITORS

This was also true of the Educational Home Visitors, who worked on housing estates where there were many young families and visited once a week at the same time with a bag of toys and activities, attempting to involve the mothers in playing and talking to their children from 6 months up to 3 years. All families who attended the programme were then promised a nursery place.

CASE STUDY

Marcia is an Educational Home Visitor on an isolated rural estate. Her first visit to Pam and her 1-year-old daughter Tracey has gone very well, and Marcia feels that the family will benefit from her support.

On her next visit, Pam greets her at the door, saying 'I'm so pleased you've come, I need to get my hair permed,' and without more ado departs at once, leaving Marcia in charge of Tracey.

1 Is this appropriate behaviour from Pam?
2 What has Marcia failed to make clear on her first visit?
3 What immediate action should Marcia have taken?
4 Is Pam a suitable parent to be on the programme?

Activity

Surf the Net to discover what other current intervention programmes are running in the UK. Write a few lines on each, noting the age group, the aims of the programme, how it is delivered and whether there are any in your area.

Resources

Useful websites

www.hmrc.gov.uk/taxcredits
www.standards.dfee.gov.uk/parental involvement
www.parentscentre.gov.uk
www.daycaretrust.org.uk
www.home-start.org.uk
www.unicef.org.uk
www.surestart.gov.uk
www.dfes.gov.uk/publications/childrensplan/
www.everychildmatters.gov.uk/aims/
www.standards.dfes.gov.uk/eyfs/

Helpline

Tax credits: 0845 300 3900

Organisations

All-Party Parliamentary Group on Parenting
Children's Legal Centre, University of Essex, www.childrenslegalcentre.com/
Citizens' Advice Bureau, www.citizensadvice.org.uk
Family Rights Group, www.frg.org.uk
Home Start, www.home-start.org.uk
UNICEF, www.unicef.org.uk

3 *FAMILY STRUCTURES*

> **This chapter covers:**
> ■ **Changes in family structure**
> ■ **Parenting styles**
> ■ **Building good relationships**

The structure of the family has changed a great deal during the last 50 years partly due to the changing role of women.

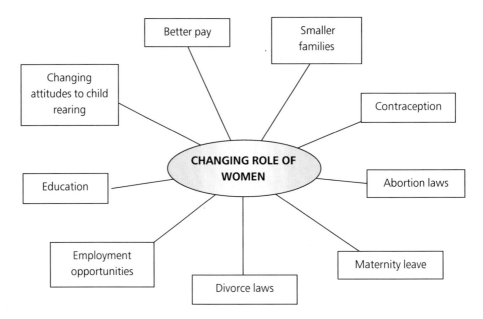

As a child-care practitioner, you will recognise and acknowledge these changes and influences and will do your best to build positive and valuable relationships with all the families within your care.

Changes in family structure

The 2001 census showed that nearly half the children in England and Wales are not being brought up in a traditional family, with their parents married and living together under the same roof. The figures show that 2,672,000 children live in lone-parent families, mostly headed by the mother. This accounts for nearly one in four of this age group.

There were 725,520 children in step-families with a re-married parent, and 1,278,455 children being brought up by unmarried cohabiting couples. A further 125,834 children were recorded as not living in a family, so the total number of children living in non-traditional households was 4,801,695: more than 41% of dependants under 18 years of age. The census also showed that more than 2,000,000 children lived in households where no adult was in work.

It is estimated that 70% of children born within marriage will live their entire childhood with both natural parents. More people are cohabiting (5% in 1986, 15% in 1999) rather than marrying and this is set to double by the year 2021. A survey of 18–24-year-olds showed that only a third thought marriage should come before parenthood. Most cohabiting relationships last less than 10 years, with 59% converting into marriages and most of the rest dissolving. The number of lone parent families is increasing. More people are living alone, the numbers having risen from 20% in 1975 to 32% in 2000. The divorce rate has risen sixfold since 1961.

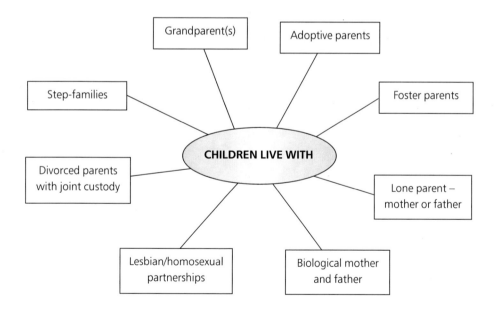

THE NUCLEAR FAMILY

This is the term for a family where children are living with their biological parents and there are no other relatives living with them. The family may live some distance from other relatives. The fact that the family unit is smaller allows the family to be more mobile, and the parents are able to accept better jobs in other areas. The expansion in university education from the 1960s has encouraged young people to move away.

Parents in nuclear families are more likely to be in higher-income professional jobs, often with both parents working. These families are more able to pay for child-care and are not so reliant on older members of the family.

Children in nuclear families may benefit from more parental attention, more space and more privacy. They may, however, have fewer people to care for them in times of stress or illness.

A nuclear family

THE EXTENDED FAMILY

This is a family where children live with their parents and have frequent contact with other family members, who may live in the same home or very close by. The extended family may consist of several generations. Family members support each other, both financially and emotionally, and spend a great deal of time together.

Extended families are more likely to be found in lower socio-economic groups, where people are less likely to move to further their employment prospects or for their children's education. Families who come to the UK from rural communities abroad, such as many of those from Bangladesh, have traditionally lived in large extended families, taking responsibility for older generations. They may feel quite isolated when settling in the UK.

Living in an extended family allows the children to experience a wide range of caring supportive relationships. On the other hand, they may feel restricted by a lack of privacy and personal space.

An extended family

GRANDPARENTS

Many grandparents look after their grandchildren while the parents work. This is particularly common when the parents are separated. It has been estimated that 24% of grandparents carry out full-time day-care when the parents live together and 44% when they do not. Most of the care is given by maternal grandparents, as paternal grandparents often lose contact with their grandchildren when parents separate. In some cases, children are living with their grandparents because of family breakdown, drug addiction, homelessness and teenage pregnancy. In some families grandparents are less willing to take on a caring role, as they may be working themselves or wish to enjoy their retirement.

Grandparents' legal rights are very limited. In most cases, where the children are being cared for full time by the grandparents, most establishments regard them as *in loco parentis* ('in place of the parents') and allow them to make decisions about the children as if they were the parents. Grandparents wishing to have legal rights should apply for a residence order under the Children Act 1989.

In times past, some children grew up believing that their grandparents were their actual parents, because of the stigma of teenage and unmarried pregnancy. This is less the case today.

LONE PARENTS

By the time of their fifth birthday, 20% of children are now living in a one-parent family, compared to 10% in 1981. In 1999 there were approximately 1,700,000 lone parents in the UK looking after nearly 3,000,000 dependent children. They make up one in four families and only 3% of lone parents are teenagers. Single-mother families have increased from 9% in 1975 to 23% in 2000. Single-father families have increased from 1% in 1975 to 2% in 2000. An analysis by the Office for National Statistics shows that more than 40% of families with children headed by a black person are lone-parent households. Among Asian families the proportion is 10%.

Lone parents are generally women who are divorced or separated from the fathers of their children. It is estimated that 50% of these fathers lose all contact with their children after living apart from them for 2 years. Some women are choosing to become mothers without a permanent relationship with a man. There is no longer a social stigma attached to bringing up children on one's own, but lone parents are often targeted in the media. The children may experience a lower standard of living and less attention at times from the parent they live with.

The government expects lone parents to go out to work as soon as possible, encouraging them by offering tax credits and some day-care places, often making them feel guilty about wanting to stay at home with their children. Various studies have shown that 90% of lone parents would like to work at some point, depending on the age of the children, the amount of financial and family support they have and their cultural perception of their role as mothers. Some women feel that working full time allows them to provide for their children, whereas others think that staying at home with their children gives them the best start in life.

Many children in lone families establish a close, warm, supportive relationship with the lone parent, and many also maintain a close relationship with the other parent.

LONE FATHERS

Some 2% of all children under 16 live with just Dad. There are around 161,000 families headed by lone fathers. Half the fathers are divorced from the mother of their children and a quarter are separated. It is rare for men to be granted custody of the children if the mother wants custody herself. Unmarried fathers are now given full parental responsibility for their children if they register the birth jointly with the mother.

The fathers may feel isolated. They may be prevented from working as it is hard to find adequate child-care and their male friends may find they have little in common with them. Most of the groups set up for lone parents are generally aimed at women.

WORKING PARENTS

In some families, both parents work, either by choice or from necessity. Many working parents feel excluded from nursery/school activities and are sometimes made to feel by the establishment that they are not pulling their weight in involvement in their children's education. The long hours spent in the workplace restrict the time they can spend with their children and what they can offer the establishment. Liaison is often through grandparents, childminders, nannies or au pairs.

STEP-FAMILIES (SOMETIMES KNOWN AS RECONSTITUTED FAMILIES)

In 2001 step families, married or cohabiting, where the head of the family was aged under 60 accounted for 10% of all families with dependent children. Increasing divorce and separation rates result in many children being part of a lone parent family that, after a time becomes part of a reconstituted family (also known as restructured or merged family), with a step-parent, generally a stepfather. There may be stepbrothers and -sisters and in time half-siblings. It is interesting to note that the number of step-families in the 19th century was as high as it is today but this was due to the early death of one partner rather than an ever-escalating divorce rate.

The National Stepfamily Association (now merged with Parentline) estimates that 1 in 12 children under 16 years old are part of a step-family, approximately 1,500,000 children, and there will probably be more step-families than nuclear ones by 2010. These families, by definition, will be larger than nuclear families and the age gaps between step-siblings and half-siblings will be greater.

Because of financial pressures, mothers in step-families may work longer hours than those in nuclear families. There may be emotional pressures in a step-family, due to jealousy within the relationship and disagreements with previous partners as to how the children are being brought up. There may be issues over maintenance or difficulties in granting access to grandparents.

Young children may well be living in two families, spending part of the week with the mother and stepfather and the rest of the week with the father and stepmother. Each family will have different customs and ways of bringing up the children, and there may be many relatives attached to each family. This can be very confusing for the children, who are coping with the outside world of pre-school or school at the same time.

All step-families come about because of loss: there is a separation, a divorce or death. If children are not allowed to express this feeling of loss there may be emotional outcomes, shown in their behaviour.

Step-families are rarer in some religious and cultural groups, such as Roman Catholics, orthodox Jews, Hindus and Sikhs, who believe strongly in the sanctity of marriage.

CASE STUDY

Hannah and Robert are the parents of Jack, aged 7. They are divorced and Hannah is now living with Charles, who is a wealthy widower and has two boys and a girl in their teens. Jack lives with Hannah and Charles most of the time, and Robert has him every second weekend and some holidays. There are still unresolved issues involving custody and access.

Robert lives alone in a rented furnished room. Jack sleeps on the sofa bed when he stays overnight. There is little room for any of Jack's permanent possessions. One Friday he bursts into tears and tells the staff in his class that he hates going to his father's. ▶

1 How should the staff respond to Jack?
2 Should the staff speak to Hannah?
3 Should the staff speak to Robert?
4 What records should they keep?

Activity
List three advantages and three disadvantages to the child of being part of a step-family.

HOMOSEXUAL PARENTS

During the last 20 years an increasing number of children have been living in households headed by lesbian or gay couples. This is partly because Government legislation was changed in 2005 when the Adoption and Children Act 2002 was fully implemented, allowing unmarried couples, lone parents and same-sex couples to adopt children.

The children could also be the result of a previous heterosexual relationship break-up after which either the mother or father has gone on to live with a new partner of the same sex. Alternatively, a surrogate mother may have been used, or in a lesbian relationship, a woman may have conceived through artificial insemination.

Although children living with homosexual parents have become more common in recent times, there can be resistance to this arrangement from some sections of society, despite all the evidence showing that the children thrive emotionally and socially to the same extent as those children living with heterosexual parents. There also appears to be no difference in gender orientation among such children.

The Civil Partnership Act 2004 came into operation in December 2005 and enables a same-sex couple to register as civil partners of each other.

ADOPTIVE FAMILIES

Adoption is the total legal transfer of a child from the birth parent(s) to other adults, giving all rights, duties and powers of parental responsibility to the adopting parents. Procedures are strictly controlled by law and the child's new status is given formal recognition by the court. A new birth certificate replaces the child's original birth certificate. Adopting parents are carefully vetted by an adoption agency and are usually childless couples, a step-parent or a natural parent such as the unmarried father of the child. Until the 1960s most children offered for adoption were young babies, but since the stigma of having a baby out of wedlock no longer applies in most cultural groups there are few very young babies available to be adopted.

A couple who want to adopt may wait an average of 18 months, and the child is likely to be at least 3 years old: over 27% of children adopted are aged 6 or more. In 2006 there were 4,980 orders for adoption. Only 253 adoption orders involved babies under 1 year. 3,200 children were adopted from care during the year ending 31st March 2008. 91% of children were adopted by couples and 9% by single adopters.

Government legislation was changed in 2005 when the Adoption and Children Act 2002 was fully implemented, allowing unmarried couples, lone parents and same-sex couples to adopt children.

FOSTER FAMILIES

Fostering a child is providing temporary care within a family, and sometimes this can turn into a long-term commitment.

Fostering can be a voluntary private arrangement. This might involve the children of:

■ parents who are studying full time away from home
■ parents who need respite from caring for a disabled child
■ parents unable to cope because of illness or bereavement.

If a child is with foster parents for 28 days or more, the local authority has to be informed in advance, even if no money changes hands. The local

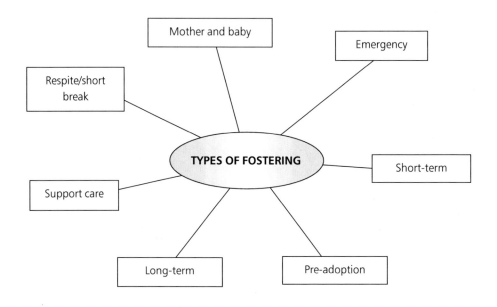

authority must be satisfied that the welfare of the child is being safe-guarded. They are entitled to inspect the home and speak to the children. They will check the foster parents with the Criminal Records Bureau, to make sure there has been no conviction for maltreating children.

CHILDREN IN CARE

There are many reasons why children are taken into care on a voluntary basis. This might be initiated by parents who feel they are temporarily unable to cope because of illness, homelessness or unemployment. The parents retain responsibility for the child, who can be removed at any time. Children may also be removed from the family home against the wishes of the parents if there has been abuse or severe neglect. Most local authorities would hope to place children with foster parents rather than in residential children's homes.

All foster carers used by the local authorities go through rigorous assessments and checks. A foster carer must:

- care for the child
- allow a social worker to visit
- notify the local authority of any serious problem
- allow the child to be removed on request
- not use physical punishment
- notify the local authority of change of address or addition of another person living at the address.

Some families foster when their own children have grown up and the parents miss having young children around. Other families foster children while bringing up their own children. Some people take on long-term fostering, with the children staying with them for many years. Others prefer short-term cover, providing a home for children in cases of emergency. The local authority pays foster carers a weekly allowance for the children placed with them.

Parenting styles

All families are unique but sociologists have noted that the way parents interact with their children is influenced by their culture, class and ethnic group, and the experiences of their own childhood. The birth order, temperament and personality of each child will cause parents to handle them differently. Children from the same family who have the same style of parenting do not necessarily develop in the same way. All families have good and bad times. Children are greatly influenced by the attitudes and parenting styles used by their parents at home.

Parents have their own ideas on how to raise children and these may be very different from the way you were brought up. How parents communicate with, relate to and discipline their children shows their ability and willingness to use their authority as parents. You need to understand about the various parenting styles. These may change as the children grow or if the family structure changes. Sometimes the mother and the father may not share the same approach, and children quickly learn who to go to for comfort, affection and security. This works as long as the parents respect each other's approach and do not seek to undermine each other.

THE AUTHORITARIAN STYLE

This is the traditional view that parents have absolute control and power over their children's lives. There are hard and fast rules and punishment is swift if these are transgressed. The parents have high expectations of their children, both in aptitude and behaviour. They tend to use physical punishment, fear and threats and are less likely to show physical affection to their children. Children are rarely allowed to question the rules.

When you are caring for children brought up in this way you may see the following outcomes:
- fear of learning, in case mistakes are made
- not admitting to any wrongdoing and lying to cover up misdemeanours

- restriction of natural curiosity, not wanting to test the boundaries
- low self-esteem and difficulty in making decisions
- a feeling that their achievements will always be inferior
- poor social and communications skills
- inability to negotiate and resolve conflict
- over-aggression towards others.

There can be a mismatch in the modes of discipline offered at school and at home, with some children unable to adjust to the less rigid regime of the school system and therefore behaving badly while at school.

THE PERMISSIVE UNINVOLVED STYLE

These parents are often coping with many pressures in their lives and find it difficult to respond consistently to the needs of their children. This difficulty may be due to a demanding job or to the pressure of coping with day-to-day living. They may not intend to be uninvolved in their children's lives but the children pick up on the fact that their parents see them as nuisances. Such parents may respond to their children inappropriately and unpredictably, swinging between harsh punishments and extravagant shows of affection. There are few routines or boundaries, the children being left to look after themselves, frequently unsupervised.

When you are caring for children brought up in this way you might see:

■ children who appear to be able to take care of themselves
■ extreme risk-taking behaviour to gain a response
■ poor self-control
■ over-anxiety to please
■ lack of self esteem – such children may become depressed.

PERMISSIVE INDULGENT STYLE

Many of these parents may have been brought up in authoritarian homes and have decided not to place controls on their children but to bring them up as 'free spirits'. These parents may be very involved with their children, showing them much warmth and affection but placing few controls on them. Such parents try to meet all their children's needs and to avoid inflicting their own standards of values and beliefs on them. Parents will often make elaborate excuses for their child's poor behaviour.

When you are caring for children brought up in this way you might see:

■ spoilt children, who see themselves as the centre of the universe and can be arrogant and demanding
■ poor self-control
■ lack of understanding and respect for the needs of others
■ aggression and disobedience
■ little understanding of limits and consequences.

THE DEMOCRATIC OR AUTHORITATIVE STYLE

Parents using this style balance their needs with those of their children. They offer their children warm physical affection alongside clear boundaries and limits for behaviour. They take responsibility for their children, setting rules and making sure they are adhered to. They expect their children to understand when they have broken the rules and to make amends, rather than punishing the children themselves. This family works as a unit, with each member having a share in the decision-making, taking age-appropriate responsibility and growing into independent, autonomous people.

When you are caring for children brought up in this way you might see:

■ children with a good sense of self-esteem
■ understanding of right and wrong
■ ability to resist temptation and accept blame
■ ability to take criticism without resorting to aggression
■ self-reliance and self-control
■ ability to form warm relationships with adults and other children.

Building good relationships

It has been said that, to build a good relationship with parents, child-care practitioners need to acknowledge that:
- 99.9% of parents love their children deeply and wish them to have the best care and education possible
- every family is unique, with its own culture and parenting style
- carers only know their own family experience and should be careful about judging others.

Schools and parents all want the best for the children in their care, and the way to do this is to work together with a consistent approach. From as long ago as the 1950s it has been acknowledged that the support and as-pirations of the parents play a vital part in the educational attainment of the children. Research has underlined the importance of parental interest, and therefore parents need to be kept well informed about their child's progress and involved in understanding the aims and ethos of the school or nursery. The child will benefit most when the triangle of parent, child and child-care practitioner works together.

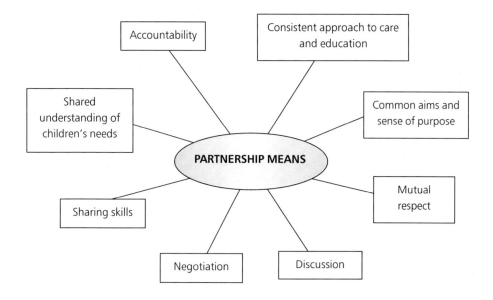

Parents spend more time with their children than any professional carer and will know their child's strengths and weaknesses, anticipate their needs and have made many decisions about their child long before the child starts any educational or care programme. Therefore, it is sensible to work with the parents in all aspects of decision-making for the benefit of the child. It will also add to the security of the child to see parents and professionals working together and in regular consultation.

Recent legislation has recognised the importance of parents as partners. For instance The Education Reform Act 1988, The Children Act 1989, The Special Educational Needs Code of Practice 2001 and The Childcare Act 2006 place a legal responsibility on all professionals in all sectors to work in partnership with parents. See Chapter 2 for further details.

An open door policy, admitting parents whenever they wish to come, is to be encouraged. Because of recent incidents when children have been attacked in schools, greater security is now necessary in all establishments and this does, to some extent, make it more difficult to involve parents on an informal basis.

Most nurseries nowadays expect parents to stay until the child has well and truly settled in. This helps build good relationships as the establishment gets to know the family and the parents gain an understanding of the routine of the setting. Research seems to suggest that, the earlier the parents are involved in the child's education, the longer this involvement lasts. Parents have many skills and much to offer the establishment and, once they feel confident, are often willing to take an active part.

Also see pages 65–66 for information about Key worker systems.

Your own attitude to the parents is crucial to building good relationships. In the past, some practitioners have been negative towards parents whom they felt had limited parenting skills. Other practitioners had a very fixed view of child-rearing practices and might have been patronising towards the parents. The Children Act 1989 stated that all families' race, religion, culture and language must be respected and that establishments are designed to meet the needs of individual families.

GOOD PRACTICE IN UNDERSTANDING VARIOUS FAMILY GROUPS

1 Be sensitive to the range of family groupings that there may be in your establishment.
2 Make sure you ascertain the structures of the families of the children in your care in a tactful and open manner.
3 Do not make assumptions about the relationships within the family.
4 Be aware of stereotypical remarks and attitudes.
5 Never be judgemental about a child's family grouping.

Resources

Websites

www.care.org.uk
www.parentlineplus.org.uk
www.fnf.org.uk
www.fflag.org.uk
www.oneparentfamilies.org.uk
www.practicalparent.org.uk

Organisations

Full Time Mothers, www.fulltimemothers.org
Gingerbread, www.gingerbread.org.uk
Home Start UK, www.home-start.org.uk
National Council for One Parent Families, www.oneparentfamilies.org.uk
Parents at work, www.workingfamilies.org.uk
Parentlineplus, www.parentlineplus.org.uk

4 PARTNERSHIPS WITH PARENTS IN ESTABLISHMENTS

This chapter covers:
- **Parents on committees**
- **Parents as customers**
- **Policies and procedures**
- **Home visits**
- **Settling children in**

The diagram illustrates the child-care and education provision where you will be working in partnership with parents.

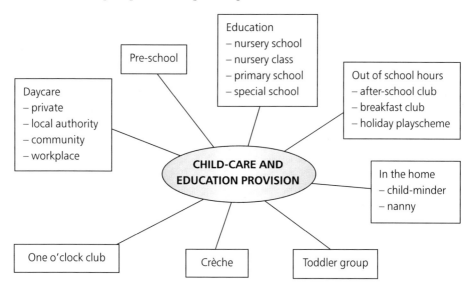

Pugh and De'ath described five categories of partnership to help professionals working with children under five evaluate their partnership with parents. These are:

- **Non-participation**: active non-participation – parents cannot be involved because of work commitments – and passive non-participation, where parents would like to be involved but lack confidence.
- **Support**: parents support the setting by fund-raising, attending events and promoting the good name of the establishment. They reinforce learning at home.

- **Participation**: parents volunteer to help on outings or on a regular basis in the establishment.
- **Partnership**: sharing in the running of the establishment with common aims respecting each other's roles. Responsibility, skills, knowledge, decision making and accountability are shared.
- **Control**: parents have the final say and are accountable for the management of the centre. This is seen in some of the community nurseries that have been set up.

As a student, using the above categories, you should be able to judge how effective the relationship is between the establishment and parents in your placement. A study by the University of Bristol looked at establishing partnerships. They identified three important elements:

- mutual support
- working together, sharing care
- power sharing, and involvement in decision-making.

It is sometimes difficult to achieve true partnership because of the power imbalance between families, parents, children and professional carers.

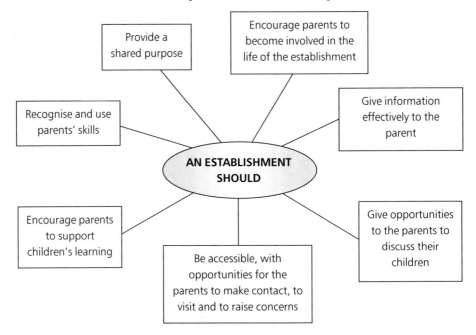

Parents on committees

Increasingly, parents are more involved as school governors or on management committees. It is important that staff and parents understand that managers define policy and staff carry it out. There needs to be a clear understanding of the role of governor/manager and which issues governors/managers should respond to as parents and which as parents' representatives. Committees deal with such things as staffing, finance, policy and curriculum. There is an obvious need for confidentiality, especially when discussing personal issues concerning staff or families. Issues about their individual child that concern parents should be addressed directly to the staff.

CASE STUDY

Josh's son is 7 and has been at the school 3 years. Josh is a newly appointed parent governor. At the first governors' meeting that he attended he asked the head teacher why his son had been sent to the 'time out' room for swearing. The head politely refused to discuss the incident.

1 Was this an appropriate query at a governor's meeting?
2 How might Josh have raised the issue so that it could be discussed?
3 Was the head teacher right to refuse to discuss it?
4 Why/why not?

In all schools parents must be given the opportunity to become parent representatives. Information should be circulated in writing. Some establishments will arrange a meeting for parents to put themselves forward for election, while others might circulate written information about each candidate.

Clear guidelines should be given outlining the tasks and duties of the elected parent. The elections should be seen to be fair and follow a published timetable. The term of office must be set out.

Activity
Ask if you might be allowed to sit in and observe during the next governors'/management meeting. Prepare yourself by reading the minutes of the previous meeting.
1 How much part did the parents take in the proceedings?
2 Were any issues raised that particularly concerned the parents?
3 Did the parents raise any new issues?

Parents as customers

In today's competitive society, schools and nurseries realise that attracting parents to their establishment is an important part of their remit. Parents are seen as customers. In early years settings most parents have heard from other parents about the reputation of the establishment, and there will be competition among the parents to enrol their child for the most popular nursery or school. In most areas, demand for child-care for under-3s may outstrip supply. On the other hand, some establishments may find it hard to attract children and may need to consider marketing their provision.

National Tests have resulted in league tables published once a year. This has led to some schools being oversubscribed and therefore many parents being disappointed.

The past 20 years have seen a vast expansion in the private day-care section, where provision is purchased by parents. These parents will expect high standards of efficiency in the running of the nursery, as well as good practice in the care and education of their child. Some may also expect to be able to communicate with the staff on any subject whenever they wish and this may not always prove to be possible. Good lines of communication are vital and important in retaining parents as customers.

Most establishments now produce a brochure extolling their strengths and explaining their aims and objectives. They often contain 20 or more pages. They give a great deal of practical day to day information, such as:

- terms and holiday dates
- hours of opening
- details of the governing body or management committee
- staffing
- collection procedures
- parental responsibilities
- student involvement
- organisation and equipment
- settling in policy
- home visits
- involvement of parents
- children's learning and the curriculum
- support staff
- planning and record-keeping
- suitable clothing
- voluntary school/nursery fund
- attendance
- illness.

The following example is taken from a brochure outlining the relation-ship between the parents and the nursery school.

Parents and the Nursery

We know that by working closely with parents each child's development and education is enhanced.

Other ways in which you can support your child and the school are:

- by taking an interest in the work the children, and your child in particular, are involved in – details are displayed throughout the school
- by spending time in the school, sharing your skills, reading with the children or helping on visits. We welcome parents reading or telling stories or rhymes in all languages
- by helping with maintaining the nursery equipment, for example making dolls' clothes or dressing up clothes, gardening or taking photographs. Please don't be shy – any help is welcomed

The Nursery

- by looking after any school pets during the holidays
- by sharing with us any anxieties, concerns and achievements.

Policies and procedures

All establishments now must have written policies and the procedures for carrying them out. Written policies exist to protect children and staff. They make sure that everyone understands the rules and the underpinning ethos of the establishment. Without policies there would be a lack of direction, with people working at cross-purposes, perhaps putting children and staff at risk.

Key policies which settings should have in place to meet current requirements include:

- **accident and emergency** – including evacuation procedures, first-aid, use of an accident book and procedures if a child is lost. Written risk assessments are also required
- **arrivals and departures** – including registration and collection procedures, and procedures followed if a child is not collected as arranged
- **behaviour** – including how inappropriate behaviour is handled
- **child protection** – including procedures if child abuse is suspected
- **complaints** – including the procedure for parents wishing to complain to Ofsted
- **confidentiality** – including how information is stored with regard to the Data Protection Acts
- **equal opportunities** – including how an inclusive service is offered
- **food and drink** – including how this is provided
- **health and safety** – including hygiene procedures to prevent cross infections, risk assessments and illness
- **medicines** – including the written permission necessary for administering medication
- **outings** – including risk assessment and parental permissions
- **working with parents** – how the setting works in partnership with families.

Activity
Ask your placement for a copy of their policy on working with parents.
1 Does this differ from those of other students?
2 Is the language simple without being patronising?
3 Is it easy to read?
4 Is it available in all the languages spoken in the placement?
5 Are parents encouraged to comment?

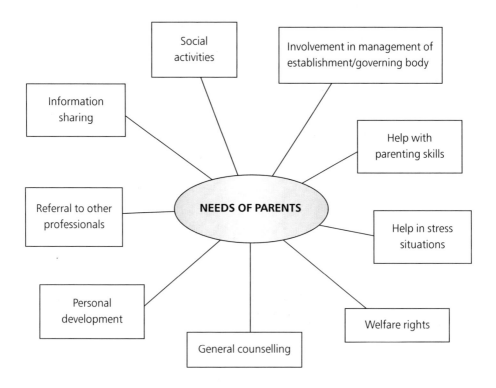

Social activities

Involvement in management of establishment/governing body

Information sharing

Help with parenting skills

NEEDS OF PARENTS

Referral to other professionals

Help in stress situations

Personal development

Welfare rights

General counselling

COLLECTING CHILDREN

Most establishments have policies about the collection of children. The National Standard *Working in Partnership with Parents and Carers* states that children should only be released into the care of people named by the parent and that, when releasing children to individuals other than the parent, the establishment needs to consider:

- making sure that parents are aware of the procedures
- obtaining prior written consent from parents as to who can collect their child
- informing parents if a child will only be released to a person authorised by them
- emergency plans, such as passwords, when the named people cannot collect a child
- where appropriate, clarifying who is the legal guardian
- regularly updating records.

The success of this policy depends on good communication between the staff and the parents.

COMPLAINTS

There are several forms of complaint. All establishments should have a policy for dealing with complaints and procedures to carry this out.

Complaints might raise issues about:

- child-care practice
- communication breakdown
- health and safety
- education policies
- allegations of abuse
- lack of customer care.

Daycare settings registered with Ofsted are required to display a copy of the setting's complaints procedures and a copy of an Ofsted complaints poster. Parents should be made aware of the course of action available to them if they have a complaint against the establishment. Parents should feel that the staff are always available to discuss any concern that they might have. If you are unable to resolve an issue you must make sure they have contact details of Ofsted Early Years Investigation and Complaint team.

It is better to avoid complaints rather than have to be in conflict with the parents. A suggestion box could be permanently sited in a prominent position so that some issues can come to light in this way, and parents can put their points of view anonymously if they so wish.

It is important to listen to parents and be prepared to discuss openly any disagreements they might have with you. If you have built up a good relationship with the parents they will trust you to listen carefully and follow any necessary procedures. All complaints should be dealt with as swiftly as possible. Records should be kept and discussed with your line manager. An example of a complaints process is shown in Chapter 10.

Home visits

Some establishments arrange for children and their families to be visited by members of staff before the child starts at the pre-school. This allows the family to meet the staff on their home ground and is thought to be less threatening to the parents than going to the establishment. Home visits are a great aid in building good relationships and involve parents right at the start of a child's education. The staff member sees how the family interacts, gets to know something about the unique culture of the home and is able to find out about the child's special preferences and needs.

The staff member will try and find out:
- how the child might react to new situations and people
- if the child is used to playing with other children
- how the child is comforted
- the home language of the child
- any special words the child might have, for example when asking to go to the lavatory

- what play activities the child enjoys
- if the child has any fears, for example of loud noises
- the level of the child's language development
- general likes and dislikes.

If the child is going in to day-care, they will also need to find out:
- the child's sleeping pattern
- dietary needs, and what are the preferred foods
- what stage the child has reached in toilet training
- the daily routine.

The staff member will have brought a booklet with them describing the establishment and will take the time to go through it with the parents, asking if they have any questions. Often, as they leave, they will present the child with a book or a small toy, to provide a home–school link.

Settling children in

If the child has had a home visit, she will have met a member of staff already. Even if this has not taken place, many schools, pre-schools and day-care centres invite children to visit their establishment with their parents before they start. All establishments will have policies on settling children in, and the procedures for carrying this out. Most will encourage the parent to stay with the child, and the length of time will depend on the age of the child, the hours the child is expected to attend and the individual personality of the child.

SETTLING-IN POLICY

Rationale

Starting school involves a major transition for the child. Young children have particular needs. When starting school they are entering a new environment which is complex and demanding of a child's growing but tentative independence.

Children bring a wide range of experiences and will be at varying stages of development.

The transition from home to school is of great significance to parents also. Fostering partnership with parents from the outset is essential to enable them to feel valued with a significant contribution to make towards their child's education and learning.

▶

This policy aims to address these needs.

Purpose
We want the children to:
- feel happy, secure and confident in the learning environment
- develop positive relationships with their peers and the adults
- feel valued by them
- become increasingly independent
- maintain and develop their natural curiosity about the world, environment and immediate surroundings
- be able to make choices
- be aware of and take pleasure in their increasing knowledge and understanding
- be sensitive to their own and others' feelings
- respect and care for their environment.

We want the parents to:
- feel valued as significant contributors to their children's development and partners in their education
- be comfortable and relaxed within the school
- feel able to ask questions, discuss and share information.

We want the learning environment to:
- be welcoming and inviting
- enable children to feel secure, to explore and to develop independence
- enable the child to feel valued both as an individual and as a member of a developing group
- be resourced to address children's overall and specific needs
- reflect children's home experiences and their cultural identity
- enable parents and children to contribute to and feel a part of it.

We want the staff to:
- work in harmony with each other
- be aware of and respond appropriately to the needs of young children, their parents and carers
- engender a warm welcoming atmosphere
- communicate with each other and parents about children's developmental needs and learning
- value the children's and parents' previous experiences
- provide information about the school's philosophy and practice.

▶

Broad guidelines

Partnership with parents should begin before the child attends the school.

This will be encouraged by inviting parents and children to visit the school on an informal basis and meet the child's key workers prior to the child's entry date. Home visits will also be arranged by mutual agreement between staff and parents.

The school's philosophy, organisation and practice will briefly be outlined and parents will be given the opportunity to raise questions and share information.

Prior to the child's starting date parents will be invited to a meeting with staff and governors to gain and share information and participate in aspects of the school's curriculum practice.

Starting dates will be staggered to ensure that staff spend time with each child and the parents.

The pattern followed and length of time needed when settling in will vary considerably between children. It is therefore essential that each new child's needs are considered and regularly reviewed by staff and discussed with parents so that difficulties can be addressed and plans agreed.

It is important that time be given to both child and parent so that neither feels pressurised during this crucial initial period.

Further information about the child's interests and experiences should be gathered by the child's key staff during the first days.

Parents should be invited to share their perception and expectations of their child's nursery education.

The time spent by the child without a parent or familiar adult will be increased gradually.

The staff room should be available for parents and with refreshment-making facilities.

A more detailed review of the child's early response to the school should take place between key staff and parent(s) after approximately half a term.

Staff will regularly observe the new children to monitor their behaviour and adapt the curriculum to take account of their needs.

▶

Children need time to form attachments with the staff. Some may choose a member of staff other than their base room teacher or nursery nurse. This is perfectly acceptable.

The staff will liaise with each other to make sure that important information is communicated.

The significance of the step taken by each child when entering the wider, more complex environment of the nursery school should not be underestimated. It is a process that requires sensitive and informed handling to ensure that the child's and parents' first days are positive, setting the scene for a constructive nursery experience.

Strategies and procedures adopted to foster a smooth transition into the nursery school

On the home visit:
- The child's interests and favourite books and toys will be discussed (staff will try to reflect some of these in the school on the child's first day).
- The child will be loaned a story book by the school to be brought back on his or her first day.
- A booklet containing annotated photographs of school activities and routines will be shared with parent and child.
- Another booklet, to which the child contributes, will be initiated. This will contain the child's name and the child's drawings. Parents and child may wish to continue with this book and bring it to share with staff and children in the first days.
- Parents will be asked to choose with their child and bring to the school a photograph to mark his or her cloakroom peg.
- The school's settling-in procedure will be outlined and the importance of giving time to this process will be stressed.
- The school's organisation and routine will be outlined and discussed.

On the first day:
- The child will come to the school about half an hour after the beginning of the session to avoid the rush and to allow the staff time to give individual attention to both child and parent.
- Usually, only one child will be admitted to each class at a time.
- The parent will be encouraged to stay with the child exploring the school environment together.
- It is accepted that the child may only want to stay at the school for part of the session.

▶

- The parent(s) will be given a booklet explaining the school's philosophy, organisation, practice and routines.

During the first weeks:
- Story sessions with a whole class group can be daunting and even frightening for a new child. During the initial settling-in period, parents will be advised to take their child home prior to the story sessions.
- As the child's familiarity with the school and confidence grows he or she will be involved in a story session within a small group.
- Many children have a favourite 'comforter' at home. They should feel able to bring this to school if it will help the settling-in process.

Points to observe to form an assessment on the extent to which children have settled into the school
- Is the child happy to come to school?
- Does the child talk about the school?
- Can s/he explore the environment independently of the parents and then the staff?
- How does s/he feel about leaving the parents?
- Which activities or experiences does s/he approach and enjoy?
- What are the child's particular interests?
- Are there any that s/he avoids?
- How does the child approach activities, e.g. persistent, confident, inquisitive?
- Which adults does s/he relate to and how?
- How does the child cope with larger group sessions, e.g. story time?
- How does the child cope with his/her self-care, e.g. going to the toilet, handwashing, putting on a coat?
- How does the child use language, e.g. to express needs, share experiences, question?
- How does s/he respond to language, e.g. simple instructions, listen attentively to stories, comment on them? Bilingual children need to be assessed in their first language. Arrangements need to be made for this, e.g. support workers, parents.
- How far have the child's physical skills developed:
  - gross motor skills, e.g. balance, co-ordination?
  - fine manipulative control, e.g. use of tools, small equipment?
- What knowledge and understanding does the child have?

Signed: Date:
Chair of Governors

Some children will have had many social experiences, in and out of the family home, whereas the experience of others may be of being one child living with a lone parent, with no extended family and unused to being with other children.

THE PARENTS' PERSPECTIVE

The parents may feel upset when their child first starts at a nursery or a school. This may be the first time they have handed their child over to other carers, and their range of emotions may include:

- guilt at leaving their child with strangers
- anxiety about the safety of the child
- the feeling that not knowing enough about child-care and education may impede their judgement of the suitability of the establishment
- doubts about a decision to return to work
- unhappiness at the thought of parting from the child
- unhappiness about possibly missing out on certain milestones, such as finding the first tooth, seeing the first steps, hearing the first words
- anxiety that other people might replace them in the child's affections
- anxiety about being able to cope with the logistics of running a home, doing a job and developing a relationship with the staff
- worry over how they will manage if the child does not settle.

Staff need to be sensitive to the feelings of the parents as well as those of the child. Staff might help parents by:

- staggering the hours the child is expected to stay
- staggering the starting days, so that the new children do not all start at once and can have more attention from the staff
- encouraging prior visits to the establishment
- encouraging parents to telephone during the day if they are concerned
- telling the parents what the child has being doing during the day
- enquiring how the child is at home after spending time in the establishment
- starting a home/school diary, where staff and the parents can share information about the child
- showing tact when reporting on milestone developments
- promising to contact parents if a child fails to settle or becomes distressed
- use of a key worker system.

When the parents are ready to leave, they should be encouraged to go quickly, telling the child that they are leaving now but will be back at a specified time, such as before dinner or after story time. The parents should never leave without saying goodbye to the child and should make a point of returning punctually, so as not to cause the child any anxiety. The way children are handed over and collected plays a huge part in influencing how they adapt to the experience in a positive way. Greeting the parents and child warmly when they arrive, making the parents feel at home and allowing them to stay as long as they wish, and making time to talk with them when they collect the child all help to build good relationships and make the family feel confident in this new environment.

Some establishments have enough room to create a parents' area, where parents can meet, have a cup of tea and have access to videos and books. Younger siblings can be brought in so that, when they start, the establishment will not seem such a frightening place. All establishments should have a parents' notice board, where information can be exchanged.

Settling in satisfactorily is most important, not least because all future transitions are affected by the outcome of the first one. This can affect moving to secondary school, going to university and even leaving home to get married.

KEY ATTACHMENTS

Babies begin to emotionally bond with their parents after birth. This gives them a sense of safety, security and love. To feel settled and secure, babies and young children also need to make attachments with other adults that care for them.

Attachments are made when familiar adults spend time with babies and children, interacting with them frequently and sensitively. The attachment felt by the child is strengthened when a familiar adult attends to their care needs. A young child will come to trust and depend on the adult to support them, both emotionally and in a practical sense.

Good care routines help children to feel cared for. For instance, when a baby is fed a bottle, they'll be held securely against the body of the adult feeding them. They receive undivided time and attention. The adult and baby will often gaze into one another's eyes. The baby may hold the fingers of the adult around the warm bottle. A feeling of closeness is shared by the adult and the baby.

So attachments form and thrive, group settings appoint a key worker for each child. The role of a key worker is to take special interest in the well-being of their key children, and to form attachments with them. Attending to children's care needs is an important part of forming such an attachment. The key worker will usually take responsible for assessing and monitoring the progress of their key children. They will get to know the family, and will be the first port of call if parents have any concerns or queries. A sense of shared care and working in partnership should be fostered between the parents and the key worker.

GOOD PRACTICE

On starting a nursery it is not good practice for too many people to handle the child.

Resources

Websites

www.governyourschool.co.uk
www.itscotland.org.uk/earlyyears

Organisations

Daycare Trust, www.daycaretrust.org.uk
Parenting, Education and Support Forum, National Children's Bureau,
　　www.ncb.org.uk

5 INVOLVING PARENTS IN THEIR CHILDREN'S EDUCATION

> **This chapter covers:**
> - **The welcoming atmosphere**
> - **Parent–Teacher Associations**
> - **Sharing the curriculum with parents**
> - **Parent education**

All parents are interested in their children's education and attainment. All research shows the benefits of schools and nurseries working in partnership with families.

The children gain confidence from seeing their parents working alongside staff. This is beneficial even if the parents involved are not their own – just having more adults around is comforting for young children, as their immediate needs can be met more quickly. Being able to have relaxed conversations with adults in an educational atmosphere helps with language development and therefore lowers frustration for the younger children. They are more able to say what they need without aggressive actions.

Parents working with the staff at school and nursery will find that it influences the way in which they help their children at home. They themselves have many skills that they bring to the establishment and from which the staff learn. The support they give to their children's learning will be appropriate and link well with the curriculum. This will also reinforce good relationships between home and school and help the family's self-esteem.

CASE STUDY

Marissa is keen to volunteer to work in the nursery class as her daughter, aged 3, has just started there and Marissa is interested in seeing what is being taught. Helen, the class teacher, asks her to sit with a group of girls who are drawing pictures of their families and to engage them in conversation.

Helen hears a commotion at the table. One of the girls, Suzy, has thrown a pencil at Marissa. When Helen asks what is going on, Marissa explains that the child had refused to finish her picture. ▶

1 What should be Helen's immediate response?
2 What has Helen failed to do?
3 What should Helen discuss with Marissa?
4 How should Helen deal with Suzy?

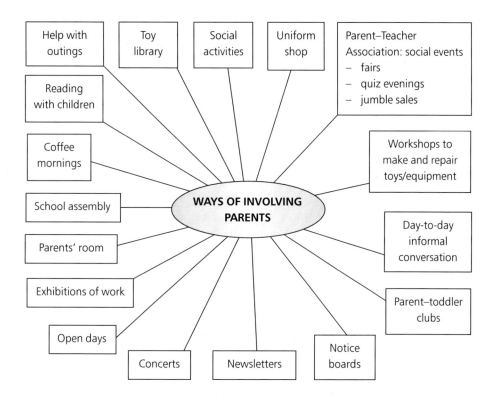

Working together in partnership allows a parent to see exactly what goes on in the classroom and how the staff cope with a large number of children. There is mutual appreciation and understanding of each other's role.

Parents benefit from working in partnership with staff in a number of ways. Many parents lack confidence initially but soon realise the value of the support they are giving and the worth of the education their children are receiving. Some then become keen to extend their own learning and education and many mature students on child-care courses have enrolled as a result of involvement in their own children's education.

Shirley's children have been at the local nursery school and Shirley has enjoyed working in the classroom. When the youngest child starts at primary school, Shirley decides to enrol as a student on a child-care and education course.

Her first placement is in the nursery school that her children had attended. Her tutor visits her and realises that Shirley is a popular member of the community and well known in the school.

1 What problems might there be in Shirley being placed in the school?
2 Should Shirley be moved?
3 What advantages might there be for the children if Shirley remains there?
4 What advantages might there be for Shirley?

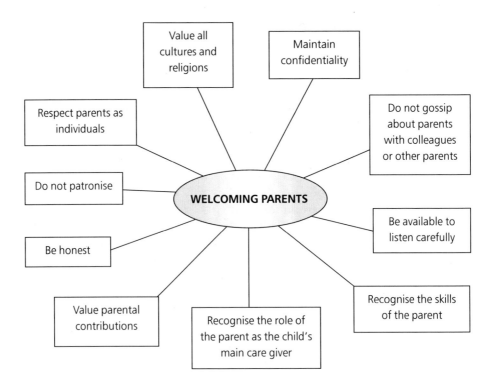

Value all cultures and religions

Maintain confidentiality

Respect parents as individuals

Do not gossip about parents with colleagues or other parents

Do not patronise

WELCOMING PARENTS

Be available to listen carefully

Be honest

Value parental contributions

Recognise the role of the parent as the child's main care giver

Recognise the skills of the parent

The welcoming atmosphere

Establishments that want parents to be involved and work with the establishment as partners need to make their building as welcoming as they can. There should be clear signs directing parents to various parts of the establishment. Both parents and staff wish to keep children safe, so there may be an intercom security system, but care should be taken to ensure that this does not act as a deterrent to parents wishing to make contact with the staff and children.

Apart from greeting each parent with a smile and having time to talk to them whenever they wish, it is vital that the school or nursery projects warmth as well as security. The building should be accessible and where possible the entrance should not be cluttered with equipment. The rooms should be attractive and welcoming. There should be

- welcome signs in many languages
- posters and images reflecting our diverse society
- photographs of staff, with their names and their role
- a notice board that parents might use to communicate with each other
- chairs for parents to use while waiting to collect children or settling their children in
- a space where parents can talk to staff privately
- time to speak informally with parents before and after each session
- respect shown to all parents.

INFORMAL SOCIAL GATHERINGS

Many establishments have informal social gatherings where staff and parents meet. They may take the form of clubs, where the whole family is involved in some craft or recreational project. Staff and parents may also get together when a member of staff is leaving, and will organise a party and collect money for a gift.

Some schools have annual fetes, run by both staff and parents, or an annual outing when the parents, the staff and the children all enjoy a day out. Many schools now hold international evenings, where parents bring food and music to celebrate the diversity of cultures in the establishment.

DROP-IN CENTRES

Many establishments run drop-in centres for families. These may be used by children and parents before starting at the school, or by parents with younger siblings. There will be toys and activities set out for the children and light refreshments for the parents, and such centres are a good way of helping families to feel comfortable in the school setting. The way that staff relate to the babies and toddlers can be a good role model for parents, who may find some toddlers' challenging behaviour hard to cope with. Ideas can be shared about how children develop and learn, respecting the parents' individual knowledge of their own children.

Some drop-in centres may have other activities on occasions, such as toy libraries from which the families can borrow toys and equipment. There may also be ideas for parents about how to use every day materials in an educational way, without going to any expense. In some drop-ins it is possible to introduce messy play, such as finger painting, which would be impractical for the parents to do at home. In some areas drop-ins are used as a resource for the local community, providing educational classes such as language support or adult literacy.

Parent–Teacher Associations

Most primary schools have Parent–Teacher Associations (PTAs). They are a key factor in building good relationships between staff and parents. It is more difficult to set up successful PTAs in pre-schools and nurseries as the children are there for a relatively short period of time before moving to primary school, but some nurseries have managed to set up home–school associations (see *Nursery World*, 4 January 2001).

Parent–Teacher Associations were first set up in the 1950s to fund-raise and give parents and staff the opportunity to work together. When money is in short supply for refurbishing and equipping schools, the PTA's role is more valuable than ever. The role of the PTA is changing in some areas, with many chasing grants or sponsorships.

Not all schools welcome PTAs, as they feel that the parents exert too much pressure, telling the staff of reforms and changes that they want made, but usually they work together very well, the PTA working as a forum for parents' concerns. Most are registered charities, with a bank account and a constitution. There is an Annual General Meeting once a year to present a report to all the parents. PTAs usually meet once a month to discuss and plan fund-raising activities. From time to time, staff may present information about the curriculum, especially when there have been major changes. The meetings may also be used to elect parent governors.

---

*F*riends
of
*F*Bowes

Parent Teacher Association

Friends of Bowes: supporting our children and our school

The next Friends of Bowes meeting is on
Tuesday 25 February 2009 at 8pm until 9pm at the school.

Come and find out what is happening at the school and what events and activities are being held to raise funds.

The following areas will be covered:
1. Apologies
2. Minutes of meeting held on 14.01.09
3. Chair's report
4. Headteacher's report
5. Treasurer's report
6. Future events and fund raising
7. Distribution of F.o.B. funds
8. Any other business
9. Date of next meeting

All parents and staff are welcome.

Sharing the curriculum with parents

Some schools and nurseries seem to be more willing to involve parents in their children's learning than others. A great deal depends on the head teacher or manager of the nursery and how important parental involvement is seen to be. Involving parents takes time, resources and effort and when staff are feeling under pressure and morale is low it is often difficult to initiate parent–staff partnerships. This is especially true in establishments where the parents are unsure of their role or staff find it difficult to relate to parents.

STRATEGIES FOR INVOLVING PARENTS

All parents are exposed to the way the establishment presents itself. Displays of work attractively mounted on walls, on tables or on chests show the parents what the children are doing and how their work is valued. A written explanation of some of the work is valuable in explaining a specific project and how it enhances the children's learning. Staff should always be willing and able to explain clearly to parents why certain work is being carried out and the value of it to the children.

Below, and on the next few pages, is an extract from a nursery school brochure.

Children's learning
We aim to encourage children to be happy, confident and independent, to enjoy learning and take pleasure in their developing skills, knowledge and understanding.

To do this, children need a safe, stimulating environment that provides opportunities to explore and experience a wide variety of materials and activities.

Children need time to **play** and **talk**, with many opportunities for **'hands on'** experience.

Play is often regarded as a light-hearted recreation – a break from real work. Play, however, is the child's approach to understanding and making sense of her or himself as an individual, relationships and the wider world. Through play, children explore, investigate, experiment and build on experience. Play provides the opportunity to practise skills and solve problems. Most importantly, play enables children to act out real and imaginary roles or situations and so grow to understand the complex and sometimes confusing world in which they live.

▶

If we are honest, adults also learn through play – many great discoveries have been made by adults at play.

Talk

Talking is of course the main means by which we all communicate. It is through talk that children organise their thoughts, understand concepts, question, express feelings and ideas and develop their imagination. Because talking is so important, many opportunities are created in school for children to talk with each other and adults.

Nursery children singing

'Hands on' experience

From a very early age, children learn through touching, smelling and observing people and materials. You will all have seen how a young baby stares at a face for many minutes and explores everything through his or her mouth.

Children need to handle objects, to explore and manipulate them, in order to build their understanding.

They also need to understand why things are done, why situations happen.

You will have noticed, also, how much young children like to copy you. In the Nursery school, we provide 'real life' resources and experiences so that the children can understand the purpose of learning.

For example, within the communication, language and literacy resource area, there is office equipment, including staplers, hole punches, diaries and note pads so that children can understand why we write.

Magazines, cookery books and newspapers are in the home corner.

The music area contains music books with musical notation.

▶

The nursery outing

The curriculum

A curriculum, based on the Early Years Foundation Stage is used within the school. This curriculum is appropriate to the children's age and stage of development.

The main areas of learning covered by this curriculum are:
- Personal, social and emotional development (which includes spiritual and moral development).
- Knowledge and understanding of the world (which includes science, technology and humanities).
- Communication, language and literacy.
- Problem solving, reasoning and numeracy.
- Creative development.
- Physical development.

In order to develop in these areas, the children will have the opportunity to:

1. Increase their understanding of the world around them by playing out everyday and imaginary situations using the home corner, dressing up clothes and small world equipment, such as play people, farm animals and train sets.
2. Listen to stories and so develop a love of literature and an understanding of the pleasures of reading.
3. Develop their drawing and emergent writing skills using adult tools including biros as well as felt tipped pens and crayons.
4. Develop early mathematical concepts through first hand practical experiences. For example, children will learn about volume and capacity by using different sized containers in the water tray.
5. Make scientific discoveries by using equipment such as mirrors, lenses, magnets, old clocks and telephones, which are kept in the science resource area.

▶

6. Develop their creative skills and imagination in the art workshop area using a range of materials such as glue, scissors, boxes, material and paint.
7. Develop their musical ability by singing and using the instruments, including a piano.
8. Develop a love of movement through dance.
9. Work out how objects fit together and balance; for example, building with bricks or arranging jigsaw puzzle pieces.
10. Handle and explore a variety of materials such as water, wet and dry sand, clay, dough, and paint. Cooking activities provide a real life opportunity to explore the changing properties of substances.
11. Learn to co-operate with others, take turns and deal with conflicts. Children are helped to do this by the staff's example and support and through games and group activity.
12. Develop their large physical skills and confidence by using the large and small apparatus in the garden.
13. Develop their small, finer movements when using small equipment and tools, such as Lego, pens and pencils.

Albums, containing photographs with accompanying explanations of children's learning are available in the staff/parents' room.

Much of the equipment is deliberately stored at child level so that children can select it and work independently.

Children love to share ideas and interests from home. We welcome these, building on them to develop the children's learning.

Please let us know about experiences or outings that have captured your child's interest and imagination so that we can talk with him or her about them.

A letter

The climbing frame

When the children go on an outing, photographs taken of the event are useful to show to those parents who are unable to come, and a display can be put up in the room. Extra photographs can be ordered if the parents want them. All establishments have to seek permission from parents for photographs to be taken of the children.

Video recordings of children working in the school or nursery, with an explanatory commentary, are a useful way of showing those parents who are unable to take part in the classroom just how the children work and how different this might be today from their own experiences. These can also be shown on open evenings, when the parents come to discuss the progress of their child. Again, permission must be sought from parents before the children are filmed. On some occasions, parents are invited to 'play' with the equipment themselves.

All schools and nurseries will have booklets giving parents information together with an outline of policies and procedures. The aims and objects of the establishment will be set out. Some schools may have more emphasis on academic work, whereas others may highlight their reputation for music and drama.

Most establishments have 'book bags' and children are encouraged to take books home to read with their parents. A record is kept by the parents and the staff of how the child is progressing. Most schools send out newsletters, keeping parents informed as to future events and so keeping them up to date. Plans of the curriculum, both long- and short-term, may be displayed in the classroom or sent home to parents.

Many nurseries have home diaries, allowing staff and parents to communicate on many aspects of the child's development. These need to be discussed fully with the parents so that they can see what is expected of them in contributing to these diaries. All establishments observe and assess the children regularly, and these records should be shared with the parents. In addition to a parents' notice board, some establishments will have a notebook in the room, in which parents can record any concerns or information.

Many nurseries will ask parents to volunteer to work in the nursery, either on a regular basis or when they can find the time. The parents might play board games with the children, initiate conversations with some of the shyer children or involve the children in construction play. Using volunteers enables the nursery to offer a wider range of activities. Some parents have particular skills, perhaps musical or artistic, and this is much appreciated by both staff and children.

Home–school Diary

This diary forms part of the ongoing dialogue between home and school. The things you tell us will inform our planning and record-keeping and help us build up an increasingly detailed picture of your child. We can let you know the sorts of things your child is doing and enjoys at school.

The diary can also be used as a means of communication if you cannot get to school to speak to us. We will read and comment on a regular basis but please feel free to write as often as you like. Please keep this diary in your child's plastic book bag, which, if brought to school daily, can also be used to transport pictures and newsletters.

---

march 19th

Theo really looks forward to the days when he stays for lunch at the nursery.
On Monday he was talking about dancers who came to the nursery + made funny noises. Was this just the children dancing?

Theo seems to have made some close friends this term, and talks about Carly, Robert, Jordan and Sophie a lot. He is very excited about the baby ....

Vicky

March 21

Yes, this term Theo has formed friendships with Jordan and Sophie He has also made good friendships with Robert from Red Room. Recently they were very busy creating a water way from crates and a bit of guttering, they then poured water down which made the boats move.

Lorna

All schools issue a report from the governors once a year. This will comment on staffing, curriculum, and building and financial issues.

In some schools parents help in the classrooms. Not all schools are as open to this as others, and not all parents are either able or willing to become involved in day-to-day activities. Parents volunteering should be checked by the Criminal Records Bureau. Some parents have particular skills that they can offer to the class, such as information technology or music. Many parents take part in hearing children read. This is much valued as it is impossible for the staff to hear all the children read on an individual basis for more than a few minutes a week. Success in involving parents in this way depends on the school and the parent. Parents need to be given clear guidelines as to what to do. Without this, many parents will lack confidence and not know what is expected of them.

Staff always value the presence of adults on outings, whether these are educational trips for older children or daily walks to the park for under-5s. All major outings need to be carefully planned and most would not take place without the help of parents. The staff will inform the children and the parents of what is going to happen, the intended learning outcomes of the trip, who is looking after which children and the need to keep alert and focused.

In nurseries, the ratio of adults to children is:
- under-2s – 1 adult to 3 children
- 2–3-year-olds – 1 adult to 4 children
- 3–5-year-olds – 1 adult to 8 children.

Obviously, the younger the children, the more help is needed. Most nurseries would expect to have 1 adult to 2 children if all the children were 3 or 4 years old and more if babies and toddlers were going on the outing as well. In infant schools, the ratio is 2 adults to 30 children when the children are in school but on an outing the class would hope to take at least 1 adult to 4 children. Parents are vital to the feasibility and the success of all school outings.

Some nurseries and schools hold workshop sessions where informal teaching may take place. Some schools offer numeracy and literacy classes for parents, particularly in areas where many families have just arrived in the UK. As well as having all written information in several languages, it may be possible to have an interpreter on hand to explain the proceedings to those families who are not yet familiar with English. Many nurseries will organise workshops so that parents may gain an insight into the early years curriculum, and videos of the children can be very helpful. On occasion, parents may be asked to help with making resources or mending books and equipment. Well planned and well run sessions help to build good relationships between the establishment and the parents.

A report in *The Independent* on 5 December 2002 stated that an inner city primary school had recently achieved a 400% improvement in its test results after offering classes for parents to help them improve their children's academic performance. They ran a range of courses from parenting skills to literacy, numeracy and computing. Truancy rates also fell.

HOME–SCHOOL AGREEMENTS

Since September, 1999 all state primary schools must have adopted a home–school agreement following consultation with parents. Parents are not legally obliged to sign the document and any breach of an agreement by either side is not legally binding. Governors are responsible for issuing any such agreement and inviting parents to sign it. Good practice would dictate that governors begin the procedure by asking parents, staff and pupils to construct a list of what they expect from the school, thus making sure the agreement reflects shared principles. Agreements will cover:

- the aims and values of the school
- the schools responsibilities in relation to all pupils
- parents' responsibilities
- the school's expectation of its pupils: this may cover behaviour, attendance and homework
- the information schools and parents may share
- the school's complaints procedure.

Bowes Primary School
Home/School Agreement

The School will:

- provide a broad and balanced curriculum and meet the needs of all children

- expect and encourage children to do their best at all times

- expect and encourage children to respect others and their environment

- provide regular homework opportunities

- arrange regular parents' consultations to discuss children's achievements and progress

- let parents know about any concern or problems that affect their child's schoolwork or behaviour

- contact parents if there is a problem with attendance or lateness

- inform parents termly about the curriculum to be followed in their child's class.

▶

The Family will:

- ensure children arrive at school on time: nursery – 9am and 12.45pm; Reception to Year 6 – 8.50am
- ensure children attend regularly and arrange family holidays during school holiday times
- inform the school about any changes of circumstances that may affect their child
- attend parent consultation evenings to discuss child's achievements and progress
- encourage their child to complete homework set by the school
- when possible, attend child's class assembly and support other school events and activities.

Together we:

- expect children to behave appropriately at all times
- work to meet all children's needs
- support the Behaviour Policy
- listen to each other and work in partnership.

Name of Child: _____Class: _____

Signed _____ Parent/Carer

Signed _____ Class Teacher or Home/School Link Co-ordinator

Date_____

Bowes Primary School – Be Included

Activity

When you are in your placement find out:
1 how the curriculum is explained to the parents
2 how many parents take part in helping in the classroom or nursery
3 if parents are able to contribute to their child's record of achievement
4 how information is shared about the child's progress
5 what workshops/meetings for parents take place during the year.

Parent education

Some parents find it hard to be good parents, while others have difficulties in their relationship with each other, which can affect the way that they parent. Other parents feel that they could do a better job with some help. Some programmes have been devised to help these parents.

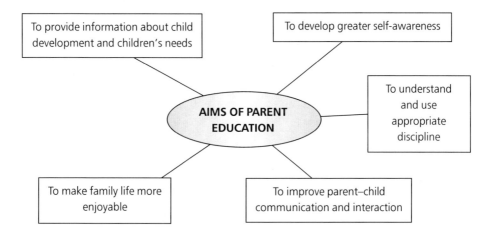

Parenting education takes place in nursery, primary and secondary schools, ante-natal clinics, infant welfare clinics, family day-care centres, drop in centres, further education colleges, adult education centres and the open university. Many parenting programmes have been published providing a model of training. Sometimes parents refer themselves as students on these programmes and sometimes they are referred by social workers, health workers, teachers or counsellors.

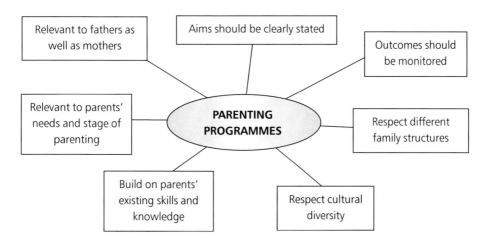

1   Welcome all parents into your establishment and treat them with respect.
2   Acknowledge that the parents know more about their children than you do.
3   Value the diversity of cultures and acknowledge the uniqueness of each family.
4   Listen carefully to what the parents say and remember the importance of good communication.
5   Consult parents before making changes.
6   Recognise and value the various skills that parents have.
7   Maintain confidentiality.
8   Avoid pre-judging families and situations, and never gossip.
9   Share information about the child and trust parents' decisions about the child's future.
10 Help parents to become a part of the school/nursery community.

Resources

Website

www.parentscentre.gov.uk

Organisations

Kids Clubs Network, www.4children.org.uk
National Confederation of Parent/Teacher Associations, www.ncpta.org.uk

6 PARTNERSHIP WITH PARENTS IN THE FAMILY SETTING

> **This chapter covers:**
> ■ Working as a nanny
> ■ Working as a childminder

Working in a family setting is very different from working in an establishment. You will have very close contact with, and responsibility for, a small number of children and so it is vital that you establish a positive working relationship with the parents.

Working as a nanny

If you decide to embark on a career as a nanny, you will soon realise how important it is to build good relationships with the parents of the children in your care, always keeping in mind that parents are the experts on their own children and respecting their values and opinions. Your relationship with the family will extend to grandparents or other relatives in frequent touch with the family.

Parents will know their child's strengths and weaknesses, anticipate their needs and will have made many decisions about their child before employing you. Therefore it is sensible to work with the parents in all aspects of care and education for the benefit of the child. It will add to the security of the child to see parents and nanny working together and in regular communication.

Activity
List the reasons why some parents prefer to use home care rather than place their child in group care.

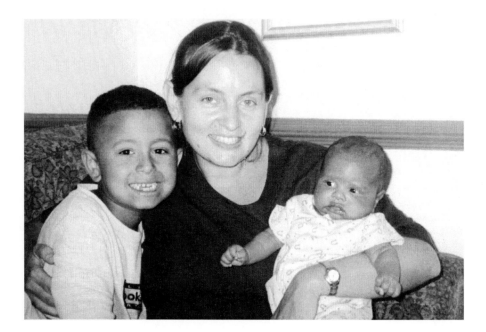

With any professional relationship, there will be a certain amount of tension and anxiety felt by both yourself and the parent/s when you first have sole charge of the child. The parents' range of emotions may include:

- guilt at leaving their child
- anxiety about the safety of the child
- the feeling that not knowing enough about child care and education may impede their judgement of the suitability of the nanny
- doubts about the decision to return to work
- unhappiness at the thought of parting from the child
- unhappiness at possibly missing out on certain milestones
- anxiety that the nanny might replace them in the child's affections
- worry (if the nanny lives in) that a third adult living in the home might cause difficulties in the parents' relationship
- anxiety about being able to cope with the logistics of running a home, doing a job, and developing a relationship with the nanny
- worry over how they will manage if the arrangement breaks down.

In addition to excitement and enthusiasm about your new role, as a nanny your range of emotions may include:

- an image of the parents as professional working people and you in a lower-status job

- fear that you will not be able to form a satisfactory relationship with the parents
- fear that you will not like the child/children
- worries about cultural and social differences
- worries that your knowledge and skills are not sufficient to equip you to do the job satisfactorily.

The parents may give you a great deal of information about the children. Equally you may find that they are new, inexperienced parents, who are not sure what you need to know. So that you may settle easily into the home, it is a good idea to complete the chart on page 88 with the parents.

CASE STUDY

Vanessa lives in with a family of three children, including a baby, as well as the parents and the mother's mother. Granny creates all kinds of problems when the parents are out at work. She overrules Vanessa's decisions, smokes in front of the children, disrupts the daily routine and constantly criticises Vanessa's skills and knowledge.

1 How might Vanessa tackle this problem?
2 Should she speak to the parents about it?
3 How might the parents react?

After a while, you will start to feel part of the family, and you should be made to feel comfortable with close relatives and accepted by them. From the start you need to talk to your employers about their families so that you know who everyone is and have some idea of how they relate to one another, and in particular to the children. If grandparents live close by you may well see them during the day without the parents being present, and will soon appreciate how much they have to offer.

Nannies should provide care that is consistent with that of the parents. Children's needs and parents' wishes may derive from a cultural or religious source, or have medical reasons, or quite simply, be what the parents want for their child. Parents' wishes and child-rearing practices must be respected and every effort must be made to comply with them.

Nannies and parents should discuss and agree about matters relating to:

- food, its preparation and eating, for example meat-free or exclusion of certain meats or other products
- table manners
- suitable activities

Home information

SECURITY

Tick box for yes.

Do you know how to secure the home (doors, windows, shutters)? ❏

Do you know how to set the alarm? ❏

Do you know where to find a spare set of keys? ❏

SAFETY

Where to find the:

Fire extinguisher ....

Torch ....

Candles ....

Fuse box ....

First Aid kit ....

EMERGENCY telephone numbers:

Doctor ....   Vet ....

Gas ....   Water ....

Electricity ....   Local authority ....

....

RUBBISH DISPOSAL

Arrangements for disposal of rubbish:

....

....

DOMESTIC EQUIPMENT

How to use the:

Washing machine ....

Drier ....

Microwave ....

Cooker ....

Dishwasher ....

Central heating ....

Other essential information ....

....

- outings
- personal hygiene
- skin and hair care
- the question of clothing during play
- periods of rest and sleep, for example routines and comfort objects
- expected behaviour and modes of discipline
- contact that the child has with other children and with friends of the nanny.

Do not assume that, because a family is part of a particular cultural group, they follow all the practices of that culture. It is essential to discuss all aspects of the child's care with the parents and find out how they wish you to care for their child.

CASE STUDY

Cynthia, a practising Christian, has accepted a post with a Muslim family where she will have sole charge of their 3-year-old daughter and 18-month-old son.

1 What will Cynthia need to ask the parents?
2 How will she demonstrate to the parents that she can provide the care they wish for their children?

Once agreement has been reached you must respect parents' wishes and stick to the practices agreed. Not to do this would represent a betrayal of parents' trust and demonstrate a lack of respect for their views and child-care practices.

Living and working in a family home may be difficult and there may have to be a great deal of give and take. You having a close relationship with the children may be hard for your employer, and you must be prepared for some ups and downs. Your relationship with your employer is crucial to the success of the arrangement, and as in any relationship the key lies in communication.

COMMUNICATING WITH YOUR EMPLOYER

Communication between you and the parents needs to be clear and uncomplicated at all times if you are to establish a harmonious partnership. You will need to be able to convey your expectations to them while at the same time listening to their point of view. Lack of communication can lead to misunderstandings and this may affect the children.

It is important to set aside a time, either weekly or daily, at which to discuss with your employer any problems that may have occurred, achievements that have been reached and any changes that need to be put in place. This may be half an hour at the end of each day to begin with, reduced to just an hour a week as you settle in. Nevertheless, don't allow this important slot to disappear altogether: the children are growing and developing all the time and you don't want the parents to lose touch with what is going on.

Communication is a two-way process, and efforts will have to be made on both sides. Always be available if your employer rings you. Sharing a daily information chart with your employer, as illustrated in the chart below, is an excellent way of helping you both to keep in touch with day-to-day events. You could use this as the basis for your daily or weekly update, going through the chart and discussing each child and their activities.

Daily information for parents	
Date	Tuesday 2 May
Sleep	Josh slept for an hour this morning.
Toileting	No accidents today!
Health	Josh seems a little off-colour today. No temp. though.
Meals	Both had cheese sandwiches and fruit for lunch and fish fingers, green beans and new potatoes for tea. Hannah still not keen on beans but she ate a small portion.
Play	Hannah and I did some painting while Josh slept this morning. We all went to the park this afternoon. Josh really likes his new football.
Social	We met Jake and Fiona at the park. The children get on well together.
New skills	Hannah can tie her shoelaces now — with help! Her painting is lovely — her faces now have noses (see corkboard). William scored 2 goals in match.
Behaviour	Both OK today. Minor squabbles over toys this morning.
Comments	The fence at the back of the garden is very splintery. Perhaps now that the weather is picking up we could get some more outdoor toys for the garden?

FAMILIES UNDER STRESS

The families of the children you care for might be feeling stress for many reasons. This might begin after you have been employed, or be long-standing. The parents may become:

- difficult to communicate with
- reluctant to meet their responsibilities towards you, such as being slow to pay you or changing your time off at short notice
- reluctant to discuss the needs of the child
- uninterested in the child's achievements
- depressed and unresponsive to offers of support
- angry and aggressive towards you
- liable to arrive home late.

A situation in the family where the child is obviously unhappy cannot be left to resolve itself. This is also true if the parents are taking advantage of your good nature and are not contributing to a positive working relationship. If you find yourself in this position you will attempt to:

- acknowledge your feelings. Seek opportunities to communicate with the parents in a non-threatening, non-judgemental manner
- be up-front and assertive. State your needs to the parents
- keep calm if you have to deal with an angry parent. Listen to what is being said and do not respond in an aggressive way yourself
- keep meticulous records of the child's behaviour and incidents involving the parents
- employ stress management techniques.

CASE STUDY

Sadie is an experienced daily nanny, who has been caring for Rosie, aged 2, for the last 3 months. She has established a good working relationship with Rosie's mother. On at least two occasions, her employer has come home very late and smelling of alcohol.

1 How do you think Sadie should handle this?
2 How can Sadie support and advise her employer?
3 How can Sadie make sure that Rosie still feels loved and secure?
4 How can Rosie's safety be ensured?

CONFIDENTIALITY

You will be expected not to gossip about your employer or anyone in the family. In fact, most job contracts you will be asked to sign contain a confidentiality clause stating that you agree not to discuss or divulge any private matters now or in the future, unless required to do so by law to protect the child from harm. This may apply if the parents have arranged for you to communicate with the school or family doctor, for example. You may well receive confidential information and you would be expected to pass that information on only to your employer.

On a personal level, spending time in the home you may become aware of domestic disagreements, business matters or difficulties with the extended family. Indeed you might find out something that could be potentially damaging to the family. You would only betray this trust if you thought the children were at risk.

If you are alone in the house, you may see private documents and correspondence left lying around, or overhear telephone conversations that are obviously private. It might be a good idea to ask your employers to be more discreet, as you wish to respect their privacy. You are demonstrating that they have selected a nanny who is eminently trustworthy and loyal.

POTENTIAL PROBLEMS

However happy a relationship you have with the family, an awareness of potential difficulties will help you to avoid them. The most frequent areas of tension include:
■ lack of clarity in the job description
■ personality differences
■ disagreements about discipline and routines
■ lack of sensitivity to your privacy
■ differences over your social life
■ not being clear as to your relationship with your family: are you a friend or an employee?
■ feelings of jealousy about the affection the children feel for you and the amount of time you are able to spend with them
■ conditions of service, including salary, time off and perks
■ the children disliking you
■ you disliking the children
■ you having no friends or interests outside the job
■ you having too many friends and interests outside the job
■ different standards of personal hygiene and general lack of cleanliness in the home.
These problem areas may be more acute if the nanny lives in.

If any of these problems occur, in spite of a full and frank interview, a job description and a contract of employment, the best way of dealing with it is to talk about it as soon as possible and attempt to reach a solution that is achievable by both of you. If you feel uncomfortable tackling an issue, the employment agency you used or your union might be able to intercede for you.

Any issue that needs to be discussed with your employer will need some thought on your part first. Spend some time discussing it with a close friend, so that you are clear about the end goal. Arrange a time to speak to your employer when there should be few interruptions. Remain calm and never lose your temper. Be ready to negotiate and show some flexibility without compromising your integrity.

The most frequent complaints from nannies about their employers are:
■ not having agreed consistency in the care of the child
■ automatically being blamed for any problem
■ not being allowed to have their boyfriends to stay
■ not having enough to eat
■ not being shown appreciation or gratitude.

If you attempt to ignore an area of conflict between yourself and one or both of the parents, the children will sense the atmosphere and may become distressed. Older children may attempt to manipulate the situation.

Sometimes, because of a personality clash or inflexible rigid ideas, it is impossible to come to an agreement and, for the sake of the children, you may decide to leave. This rarely happens, if enough time and effort have been put into the interviewing and selection process.

Working as a childminder

Childminders offer quality child-care and education. If this is your career choice, you need to realise that childminding is a very valuable service but also a business. Establishing a good local reputation is important and your relationship with the parents is vital to your success.

As with any professional relationship, there will initially be a certain amount of tension and anxiety felt by both yourself and the parents. The parents' range of emotions will be similar to those of a parent employing a nanny and leaving their children with someone else.

You, as a childminder, will also have some reservations about the new children you are about to care for. You might also feel anxiety at a stranger's reaction to your home and worry about balancing the needs of your family with those of the child you are about to mind.

The parents may come with a lot of questions and information for you, but equally you may find that they are new, inexperienced parents, who are not sure what to ask.

Becoming a childminder means that you are starting a business. You are a self-employed child-care and education provider, free to decide your own rate of fees and working conditions. For any business to be successful, it needs to be well organised, with good systems of record-keeping. You need to be sure that the parents are satisfied that you are doing a good job and that they understand and are happy with their contracts.

THE CONTRACT

The contract is important to both you and the parents of the child. It is not a contract of employment. You are providing child-care for a negotiated fee under an agreed set of terms and conditions. It outlines clearly in writing what is expected from you and what is expected from the parents. Using a contract will prevent any disagreements and put the partnership on a professional basis.

It is important that an opportunity is taken to sit down with the parents and complete the contract together, so that both sides are quite clear as to their commitment. It is also an opportunity to discuss your child-care practice and to discover if the parents have any strong preferences about the way you care for and educate their children. You should make it clear to the parents that, whatever views the parents have about smacking children, this is not an option for you. It is illegal for you to physically punish a child, and you must never frighten or humiliate children.

Once all the details have been discussed and agreed, the contract should be signed and dated by all parties. It is then a legally binding document. There should be a separate contract for each child in the family. Make a note in your diary when the contract is due for review, and give the parents adequate notice of this date. Explain that you may review your charges at this time.

If there is to be an initial settling in period, a temporary contract will have to be drawn up to cover that period.

Activity
1 Describe how you could make a good relationship with parents who have a different first language from you.
2 How do you work with parents to promote the child's confidence and self-esteem?

FEES

What you charge is up to you. You are embarking on a highly skilled career and should be rewarded for your expertise. There are factors that you need to take into account. For example, if you live in an area of high unemployment, the demand for your services may be limited and you might be in competition with a number of experienced registered childminders. If you live in an area where most of the families around are dual income professional families, you might find your services in great demand. It is also important to realise that your household expenditure will increase.

The contract should make clear what payment you expect for:
- absences of the child
- holidays (the parents' and yours)
- illness (the child's, the parents' and yours)
- older siblings
- playgroup, outings and other extras

- food, nappies, etc. (whether costed into charges or charged separately)
- part-time or unsocial hours
- retainers, including holiday retainers.

The contract should also make clear when and how you will be paid by the parents. In general, it is prudent to expect payment in advance. Never allow debts to mount up, and expect payment on the day agreed.

CASE STUDY

Cheryl, who has just registered as a childminder, looks after two of her own children, as well as Sam, aged 3. For the first 2 months, Sam's mother paid her fees regularly at the start of each week. For the past 2 weeks, however, she has given continual excuses for not paying: she hasn't got her cheque book with her; she forgot to draw out cash from the machine, and so on.

Cheryl feels very anxious, as she has not been paid for 2 weeks. Her partner has been nagging her, saying that childminding is not a charity and she must be more business-like. On Monday Sam's mother says she has forgotten her cheque book and offers half a week's fee in cash.

1 What should Cheryl's immediate response be?
2 How can Cheryl prevent money matters spoiling her relationship with Sam's mother?
3 How can she make sure she gets paid on time?

INSURANCE

When you become a childminder, you will need to review all your home and car insurance policies, and inform the companies of your new status.

Public liability insurance is a requirement of registration and insures you against legal liability arising from accidental injury or death to any person, including any minded children in your care, caused by your action or negligence, and any damage caused by the children in your care to other people's property

RECORD KEEPING

Childminders have a responsibility to know as much as possible about the children and their families. Much of this information is gathered during the first meeting with the parents. You will need to keep all the information you have about the child in a confidential file, secure from other people. The records on each child should include:
- name as shown on the birth certificate
- name the child is known by
- date of birth
- address
- telephone number
- names of parents and where they can be contacted
- emergency contact name, and where s/he can be contacted
- information about the child's health
- information about any allergies
- information about child's immunisation status
- doctor's name, address and telephone number
- name and address of any person allowed to collect the child
- written permission from parents to seek medical help in the event of an emergency.

You should also keep a record of the name and address of any person who assists you, and any person living on the premises, and be prepared to notify Ofsted in writing of any changes. When one of your own children reaches the age of 16, you will need to notify Ofsted for their records.

The other documents that you will always have to hand will include:
- your registration certificate from Ofsted
- your public liability insurance certificate
- registers of attendance, perhaps the most important document, which must always be kept up-to-date
- contracts between you and the parents
- forms signed by parents, giving permission to take the children on outings and to give medication

- an accident book, recording all the accidents occurring to the children and any first aid given, which needs to be countersigned by the parents
- records of observations and assessments of the children
- weekly menus.

Parents should have access to all the above records concerning their child. Ofsted will inform you of what it wishes to be recorded and what will be checked at the annual inspection.

GOOD PRACTICE IN WORKING WITH PARENTS IN A FAMILY SETTING

1 Respect all parents as individuals and learn from them different ways of child-rearing. Their practice may be different from yours but is no less valid. Be open to a variety of opinions.
2 Respect parents' values, practices and preferences.
3 Contribute to a welcoming and relaxed atmosphere in the home.
4 Try and communicate at the end of the day the important aspects of the child's day, sharing negative and positive situations alike.
5 Be professional at all times. Never gossip about parents to other people. Refuse to listen to unsubstantiated hearsay.
6 Offer reassurance and encouragement to parents, always emphasising the central role they play in their children's lives.
7 Be clear about your role. The more time you spend in discussion with the parent prior to working with the family, the less likelihood there is that there will be problems.
8 Always agree a contract with the parents as soon as possible, so as to avoid conflict later on.

Resources

Website

www.ncma.org.uk

Organisations

www.voicetheunion.org.uk

7 ANTI-BIAS PRACTICE

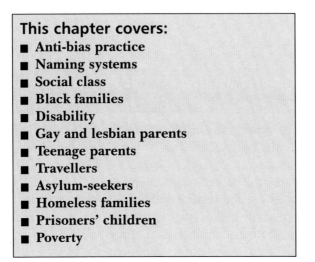

This chapter covers:
- **Anti-bias practice**
- **Naming systems**
- **Social class**
- **Black families**
- **Disability**
- **Gay and lesbian parents**
- **Teenage parents**
- **Travellers**
- **Asylum-seekers**
- **Homeless families**
- **Prisoners' children**
- **Poverty**

Each and every family is unique, yet the children all have the same basic needs. These needs are met in different ways, depending on many variables, such as class, culture, religion, education, health, age and the environment.

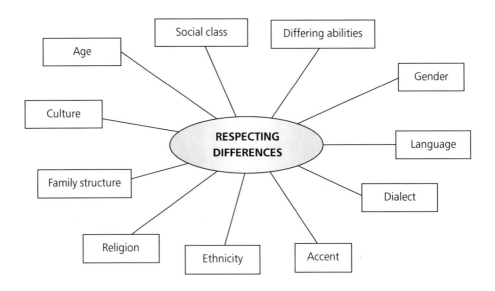

The way that they themselves have been brought up has some influence on the way parents raise their children, but the individual personalities of parents result in different parenting approaches. The influence of role models in the home will have the greatest impact on the child, yet children in the same family, treated in the same way, will not necessarily behave like their siblings. You, as a child-care practitioner, need to be aware of various family groups, and the influences within the family and your practice must be anti-discriminatory. All parents should be treated with equal concern and respect, acknowledging that they all have individual needs and strengths.

Anti-bias practice

All members of society should be valued whatever their race, gender, class, culture, age, religion, disability, or sexual orientation. This is especially important for those people working with young children and their families, some of whom face daily discrimination and abuse. It is difficult to build a collaborative relationship with parents who, because of prejudice and racism, lack self-confidence and self-esteem. Establishments recognise the negative impacts of discrimination and inequalities and have an obligation to produce anti-bias policies, which should be available for you to read.

CASE STUDY

One of the parents asked a child-care student if there were any birthdays being celebrated that week. When Jayshree, the student, said that it was Andrew's birthday on Thursday, the parent said, 'Well, I won't bring Hannah in that day, then'. On being asked why, the parent explained that the family were Jehovah's Witnesses and that they did not believe in celebrating a special day for anyone.

1 How should Jayshree respond to the parent?
2 How do you think the placement should handle this in the short term?
3 What do you think should happen when there is another birthday?

Since the Children Act 1989, anti-discriminatory practice is required by law in all establishments where there are children. The child's religious, racial origin, cultural and language background needs to be taken into account when planning the curriculum and care routines. This practice should help to promote positive images and give the family confidence. Challenging prejudice is a major responsibility for all child-care and education practitioners.

Naming systems

Many of the families in your placement may have names that appear to be similar. You need to be aware that some cultural and religious groups have different ways of naming their children.

Most European Christian children have a first name, possibly a middle name and a surname, in that order. It is important not to impose this system on other groups of children, as this would be disrespectful.

African names will differ from one ethnic group to another: for example, in the Igbo language of Nigeria the first daughter is always called Ada, literally 'daughter'. Other groups name their children after the circumstances in which they were born. Traditionally, Africans do not have a family name, but most Africans in Britain will have adopted a surname that can be used for formal documentation.

The Chinese and Vietnamese communities use the family name first, followed by the middle name and then the personal name. Children take the family name of their father. Some have now reversed the order of their name to follow the British pattern, so care should be taken when filling in records.

Muslim boys of Pakistani and Bangladeshi origin often have a religious name before their personal names. Calling such a boy Mohammed or Abdul, without adding the personal name, may well cause offence to observant Muslims, whereas in the Middle East Mohammed is a common personal name. Traditionally there is no shared family name, but to conform with British naming patterns some families have adopted a surname. Many Muslim women have, in addition to their personal name, a title such as Begum, Bibi or Nessa, which indicates that the person is female.

Sikhs place the personal name first. Singh, meaning 'lion', is a common title for men, Kaur, meaning 'princess', for women. It would be inappropriate to address a Sikh mother as Mrs Singh or her husband as Mr Kaur. In Britain, some Sikh parents give their children a first name and a surname only.

British Hindus place the personal name first. The Hindu surname is a shared family name indicating a family's traditional status and occupation.

If you are not sure how to address a child or a parent, ask. You would not like to be referred to continually by the wrong name. Remember that many names have religious or cultural significance.

GOOD PRACTICE IN ANTI-BIAS PRACTICE

1 Present positive images in your choice of books and activities and in the use of equipment.
2 Present yourself as a good role model.
3 Admit what you do not know, and be prepared to ask for help and advice.
4 Challenge all offensive remarks, whether from children or adults and whether directed against yourself or others.
5 Make sure you pronounce and spell all the children's names correctly.
6 Make sure you know the names of the clothes that the children and their parents wear.
7 Understand the different skin and hair care needs of all the children.
8 Make sure you understand the importance of a varied diet that does not go against any cultural or religious taboos.
9 Challenge stereotypes.

All parents should feel that their culture and religion is respected by the establishment. Groups of children from just one culture should also have the opportunity to know about other cultures and understand that we live in a multicultural society. You should never make assumptions about families but seek accurate information from the parents.

CASE STUDY

Natasha, the group leader in an urban day centre, asks Ada to bring in a Nigerian dish to celebrate a multicultural evening. Ada is taken aback, explaining that neither she nor her parents have ever cooked any Nigerian food and that, in fact, she does not like it.

1 Is it a good idea to link a food to a certain culture?
2 How could Natasha be sure that the family cooked food specific to their culture?

Social class

Social class has an important influence on how we view other people and how we ourselves are seen. Historically, the jobs available to the working class have demanded little imagination or creativity and have needed good manipulative skills. Rules have to be obeyed in the workplace, and there is close supervision. Occupations of the middle classes ask for different skills. Professional people are expected to work on their own, show initiative and creativity and take responsibility for their decisions. Some values, such as honesty and respect for others, are shared across the classes.

In the past, these occupational differences have had an influence on how the children were brought up. Many working-class families would expect obedience without explanation, obeying certain rules and punishing the children when the rules are broken. Middle-class parents are assumed to value curiosity, self-control, autonomy and regard for other people. These parents question a child as to why she behaves in the way she does and will often give the child some 'time out' to think about it and to reflect on the consequences.

Most parents have ambitions and aspirations for their children, whatever their background, and expect their children to have access to the best education leading to skills and meaningful employment.

During the last twenty years or so there have been many occupational changes. No job is secure for ever and jobs in manufacturing have declined alarmingly. The unions have less power and these days many working-class families have access to a life style previously enjoyed only by the middle classes. For example, many families these days have a holiday abroad, can afford to dress well, and eat out. The boundaries between the classes are less distinct, even in the way that people speak. There are still some measurable differences, for eample babies born to parents in manual work are more than twice as likely to die in the first year of life as those born to the professional classes.

Black families

Care has to be taken in not seeing black families as one group. They are, as in all families, unique units, with various cultures, customs and religions. If this is not recognised, parents will be discouraged from playing a part in the life of the nursery or school, and may feel anxious for their children. They need to be reassured that the establishment has a positive approach to anti-discriminatory practice.

Many black families find it difficult to work in true partnership with the staff in the school or nursery because of their own experiences of racism in the wider society. There may be assumptions among the staff that devalue the culture and customs of many black families. This may be even more the case when English is not the first language.

The experience of each family is different but many black families are subjected to racism and discrimination, resulting in insecurity and fear for their children's physical safety, emotional wellbeing and achievement in school. In spite of all the problems they face, most families have many strengths, for some in their religious beliefs and spiritual values.

African–Caribbean families are often headed by the mother, who successfully brings up the children as well as holding down a full-time job. These families depend on neighbours, extended family relationships and friends for support. There is often strict discipline in the home, and the children are expected to acknowledge and respect parental authority.

Families from the Indian subcontinent often live in extended families, with three generations at home. Grandparents are respected and revered for their knowledge and experience.

Some schools still do not appreciated how valuable it is being bilingual, and sometimes are not aware of the richness of the child's home culture.

Disability

A parent with an obvious disability may find that s/he is rarely included in the day-to-day life of his/her child's nursery or school. This may be because the staff assume that it would either be too onerous for the parent or dangerous for the children. The parent may feel that the access to and around the building is limited and there may not be adequate toilet facilities. Such parents fear that they might face discrimination from other parents and that their children might suffer.

The social model of disability challenges the traditional medical model and is challenging people and establishments to be more inclusive in their approach. The medical model of disability sees disabled people as a problem, focusing on what they cannot do. It labels the person as ill and in need of treatment, leading to dependency on others, which, in turn, can lead to overprotection and isolation. The phrase 'suffering from' is frequently used. The medical model reinforces reliance on others, giving disabled people no control over their lives and denying them opportunities for choice.

The social model came about from the disability movement, seeking equal rights and opportunities for disabled people. It rejects the medical model of disability but does not deny the need for medical care. It is society that is the problem, not the disabled person.

Problems are seen to lie with:

- the way society is organised, segregating special provision, funding treatment rather than resources to reduce the effect of disability, excessive influence of health-care professionals and costly special equipment
- the way the environment is constructed: physical barriers to mobility and communication barriers with little access to braille and sign language
- people's attitudes and assumptions.

The social model acknowledges those with disabilities as people first. It emphasises the need for environmental and social change to allow disabled people to live in a society that is inclusive, accessible and supportive of personal rights. Impairments are a fact of life but, if they are planned for and resources are allocated well, they do not have to become a problem.

Activity
List some assumptions that people may have about disabled children. How does this affect their attitude?

Unless a child is severely disabled she will be educated in a mainstream school and included in all the school activities. It is an opportunity for the school to educate disabled children, as it helps children and staff to get to know the disabled child as a person and to see the child and not the disability.

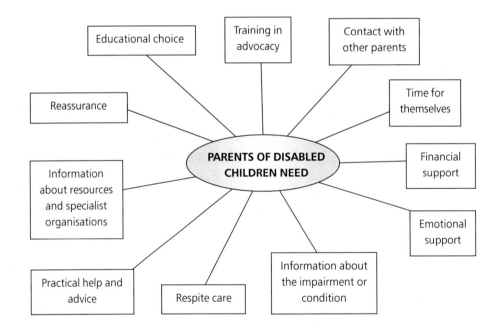

People working in early years settings may see the parents of a disabled child as being over-protective. Other parents may not wish to mix with these parents and may make them feel unwelcome. It is often impossible for parents to get a nursery place for a child who is not toilet-trained.

A report in 2002 from Barnardos called *Still Missing Out* shows that families with a disabled child often face financial hardship. The costs of raising a child with severe impairments are three times the average. The study shows that two-thirds of families with disabled children are in the bottom 40% income band. Disabled children are more likely to be born in to poorer families and their parents are less likely to be in full-time work, because of intensive caring for the children.

CASE STUDY

Inge is a teacher in a reception class. She passes by the parents' room and hears a heated discussion taking place. She asks the parents what the discussion is about and, after some hesitation, is told that the inclusion of Jane, a child who has Down's syndrome, in the class is worrying some of the parents as they feel that Jane might hold the other children back.

1 What should be Inge's immediate response?
2 Have the parents any justification for their concern?
3 Should Inge speak to Jane's parents?
4 What can the establishment do to inform the parents about inclusion?

The Warnock Report (1978) considered that parents could only be effective if professionals took notice of what they said and how they expressed their needs, and treated their contribution as important. Parents of disabled children are often under stress and may well be involved with many agencies and professional people, experiencing various degrees of support. It may well take time for you to form a constructive relationship.

It is important for you to understand that you may not be able to meet all their needs and that, in order to support the parents of disabled children you will need to know when and how to refer them on to other, more specialised, agencies. Inform yourself of the relevant helplines, websites and organisations available for support and advice.

The Special Educational Needs Code of Practice emphasises a greater need for parental involvement. Parent partnership services provide support and advice to parents whose children have special educational needs. They provide accurate and objective information on the full range of options available to parents, helping them to make informed choices about their children's education. If parents want an independent parental supporter, the service should proved one.

Gay and lesbian parents

Even in these more enlightened times, gay and lesbian couples often face discrimination in the workplace and the legal system. Children of these couples may be abused and subject to name-calling. The school or nursery needs to be a positive experience for them, and any abuse from the children or other parents should be immediately challenged by the staff.

The parents should be welcomed and made to feel that the staff will support them and their children.

Teenage parents

The UK has the highest rate of teenage pregnancy in western Europe. At the beginning of the century over 40,000 babies were conceived by girls aged 14–17 years, about half of which ended in abortion.

Some teenagers have a great deal of support from their families and, if still at school, most will carry on with their education, with a member of the family taking on a great deal of the responsibility for the baby. Others may have less support, and the establishment can be a place where the young mothers can seek advice, help with parenting skills, referral to support services and knowledge about child development. Access to child-care is often crucial in allowing teenage mothers to carry on with their education. A new government initiative 'Care to Learn?' will provide funding towards registered child-care costs.

Travellers

The term 'travellers' is used to describe various groups. There are 150,000 British Gypsy travellers, about half of whom are nomadic. Some refer to themselves as 'Gypsies' but others dislike the name. There are also New Age travellers, who are people who do not wish to participate in society and travel around in groups, and an unknown number of foreign travellers seeking asylum.

Nomadic travellers are only permitted to stay on specific sites, thus forcing some into fixed housing or illegal camps. Only one-third of travellers' children attend school and their attendance is often very patchy. In the European Union it is estimated that about 2,000,000 traveller children are being denied the basic right to an education.

Travellers' children do face discrimination. Those children who go to school are frequently subjected to abuse from other children and their parents and this discourages many children from attending school. Establishments with strong anti-discriminatory polices and procedures can be a haven of stability for children and parents, and these staff will be quick to challenge any abuse that the family receives.

Traveller parents are protected from being penalised for their child's absence from school if a parent carries out a business that requires travelling from place to place.

Asylum-seekers

An asylum-seeker is someone who has crossed an international border in search of refugee status. To be recognised as a refugee a person must have left his/her own country and be unable to return to it owing to a well-founded fear of being persecuted or even killed for reasons of race, religion, nationality, membership of a particular social group or political opinion.

The majority of asylum seekers in Britain come from countries such as Iraq, Sri Lanka and the Balkan states, where there is considerable political unrest and persecution. They may have a difficult time proving their refugee status, and are often discriminated against in the place where they are living. They face inadequate housing, often in temporary accommodation. There is a policy of dispersal to areas where there may be little family support. Welfare provision is patchy, and the families are often resented by the community.

Asylum-seekers frequently figure in political debate and create a great deal of media attention. For this reason, families and children in the schools often suffer abuse from other families and sometimes from the children. Many of the families have witnessed violence, experienced the loss of their home and of other relatives and now face major cultural changes and the need to learn a new language. As with travellers' children, it is up to the staff to protect the children as far as they can from abuse.

Homeless families

Shelter, the charity that helps homeless people, has found that there are approximately 100,000 homeless children in England alone. Government figures revealed that 78,000 homeless households are currently living in temporary accommodation, 1,000 of these in 'bed and breakfast'. Often, the whole family lives in one room. Homeless families may be affected by:

- not having enough space for play or homework
- contact with drugs and prostitution if living in a hostel
- disruptive sleeping patterns
- poor diet
- unhygienic conditions
- damp, cold conditions

- depression
- poverty
- difficulty in registering with a local GP
- facing the stigma of being homeless, and not being able to invite friends home.

Often these families are tired and experience poor health. The parents may be demoralised and unable to liaise adequately with the nursery or school. Families tend to be moved around frequently and this can result in many changes of school and impacts on the achievement and behaviour of the children. This makes it difficult for the children to maintain friendships.

Prisoners' children

At least 125,000 children have a parent in prison and this affects them in many ways. The sudden withdrawal of a parent is confusing and alarming, particularly when the remaining parent is reluctant to reveal what has become of the other parent. The family may have to move to be nearer the prison, so that the inmate can be visited. The family income will be reduced.

The impact on the family is the greatest if the mother is imprisoned, especially if the children are young. It has been estimated that 30% of women in prison have children under the age of 5. Many women are pregnant when sentenced. Depending on where they are imprisoned, their babies can stay with them for between 9 and 18 months, but there is no automatic right for the women to go into a mother and baby unit, as it is thought that some mothers might pose a risk to the other babies there. Most of these babies are then fostered, either by the family or through social services.

Not all schools or nurseries know that one of the parents is in prison. Mass media stereotyping contributes to the lack of accurate information and leads to discrimination. If staff are told that a parent is in prison, there is a need for strict confidentiality. The child and the other parent should never be questioned, and the staff should adopt a non-judgemental approach.

Activity
Ask to see the equal opportunities policy in your placement. Are all the groups mentioned in this chapter included?

Poverty

Poverty is relative to the country in which you live. In the UK, if the family income is half or less than half of the average wage, the family is deemed to be poor. It is estimated that between 3,000,000 and 4,000,000 families are affected by poverty. Poverty results in families living in substandard accommodation, which may be damp and have inadequate heating, which in turn leads to poor health. Diets are inadequate and there is little money for clothes and social activities. Transport is expensive, or non-existent in some areas, thus restricting employment opportunities.

Children in poor households attend school less often than others, resulting in fewer educational opportunities. Intellectual development differences between middle-class children and those from poor families can be seen at 22 months. This gap widens during the primary and secondary school years. Poor children are one-third as likely to get good exam results as their wealthier peers.

Poverty affects:

- birth weight
- housing
- health
- diet
- credit rating
- death rate
- stress levels
- educational achievement
- social relationships
- enjoyment of the good things of life and results in stigma, isolation and exclusion.

In poor areas, crime flourishes. Most burglaries are committed against the poor, who cannot afford to protect their property adequately and usually have no insurance.

Most staff know if a family is poor, as they often cannot take part in outings and find it difficult to give money for various fund-raising activities. The staff can help by not making this obvious to other families and by funding some of the activities from a special fund.

The present government has vowed to reduce the number of poor families. Extending the Sure Start programme to all areas of the country might help address some of these inequalities.

Activity
List the ways in which a low income prevents a family from being fully involved in an educational establishment.

1 Listen to children and their parents if they show signs of distress. Give them time and take what they say seriously.
2 Contact agencies and the voluntary sector to obtain information for yourself. You may be able to pass this on to the families.
3 Understand the process of separation, attachment, loss and bereavement.
4 Maintain strict rules of confidentiality.
5 Develop skills of observation.
6 Know when to refer a family to another agency.
7 Show respect and empathy with the families.

Resources

Websites

www.cre.gov.uk
www.bcodp.org.uk
www.eoc.org.uk
www.disabledparents.net
www.bbc.co.uk/religion/tools/calendar

Organisations

British Council of Disabled People, www.bcodp.org.uk
Commission for Racial Equality, www.equalityhumanrights.com
Contact-a-family, www.cafamily.org.uk
Disabled Parents Network, www.disabledparentsnetwork.org.uk
Young Minds, www.youngminds.org.uk

8 CONFLICT WITH PARENTS

> **This chapter covers:**
> - **Irresponsible parents**
> - **Addictive parents**
> - **Abusive parents**
> - **Custody issues**

Research shows that, when parents share the same values, aims and ethos as the school or nursery to which they send their children, the parents are more involved in the establishment and the children are happy and achieve well. Most parents try hard to find schools and nurseries for their children that share their child-rearing philosophy. In some areas, however, there is not much choice of school or nursery, and this can sometimes lead to conflict.

All families are unique and have various ways of coping with life. With many families you will share the same values. You will find these parents easy to communicate with and will share a common approach to child-rearing and education. You may find it more difficult to relate to parents who:

- push their children too hard and have unrealistic expectations of their children's achievement
- over-protect their children, not allowing them to participate in the full range of school or nursery activities, and seem to encourage a fearful attitude towards the world
- abuse or neglect their children.

You will still do your best for all the children, and by your example may be able to help the parents understand that their behaviour is not helpful to the child.

The vast majority of parents want to do their best for their child but will sometimes have difficulty in coping with their lives and this can interfere with them meeting the needs of their children in a satisfactory manner.

CASE STUDY

Melanie, aged 3, goes to a Montessori nursery school. She is a bubbly attractive child and her mother, Deborah, takes a great deal of pride in her achievements.

After half term Melanie appears tired and out of sorts. The head of the school asks Deborah if Melanie has been unwell during the holiday. Deborah replies that she is rather concerned herself, as most of the holiday has been spent in encouraging Melanie to write her name and learn to read, as she would be going to school in a year and needed these skills, especially with National Tests looming on the horizon. Melanie was often unwilling to participate and Deborah has been thinking of taking her to her GP.

1 Is Deborah right to be preparing Melanie in this way?
2 What advice should the head give Deborah in the short term?
3 What advice should nurseries give to parents about preparation for primary school?

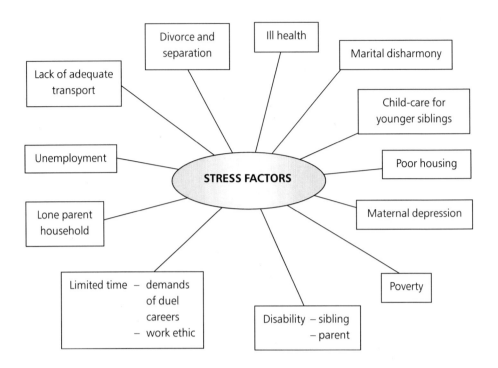

Irresponsible parents

There are sometimes good reasons why parents keep their children off school. This could be because of:

- illness
- dental and medical appointments
- close family bereavement
- referral for assessment at a clinic.

A responsible parent will give the establishment good written notice of any appointments and will let the school know immediately if their child is too ill to attend. This is then recorded as 'authorised' absence. Where parents fail to inform the school, the absence is noted as 'unauthorised'.

There could also be occasions when the parent does not agree with her child attending a session at the school or going on a visit. For example, the parent might not want her child to travel on the Underground because of the fear of terrorism, or she might disapprove of her child celebrating a festival of a faith different from that of the family.

Children are not permitted to be absent from school because they are on holiday. Families must take their holidays out of term time.

Truancy is rare in young children but, if there are many unauthorised absences, this can lead to difficulties in the relationship between the parent and the school. Some parents feel that it is justifiable to keep their children off school for:

- birthdays
- shopping trips
- visits to family
- very minor ailments
- nice weather.

Sometimes the parent finds it hard to get out of bed in the morning, and continual lateness causes a great deal of conflict. The teacher has to stop what she is doing to deal with the late child, and may become obviously annoyed with the parent, who then feels that they would rather stay at home than get told off.

Some children show extreme reluctance to go to school, often complaining of headaches or stomach aches. This could have several causes:

- there are problems at home
- the parent is unwell and the child does not want to leave them
- the child is being bullied or made fun of at school
- the child is really unwell.

It can happen that a child is sent to school or nursery when the parent knows her to be unwell. This is unfair on the child, as she is unable to take a full part in the school day, and it is unfair on the establishment, who will have to care for her and be at risk of the spread of infection. The staff might have to spend time contacting the parent in order to collect the ill child. Medication cannot be given to a child by the establishment unless written permission is given.

Parents who pay for their child-care, such as those who employ nannies, use childminders or send their children to private establishments, can cause conflict through late or non-payment of fees. Systems of payment should be made clear to parents from the start so as to avoid problems.

Lateness in collecting children causes a great deal of conflict in nurseries and schools. It means that a member of staff has to remain on site until the parent or carer arrives. The child often becomes very upset, especially if the person in charge shows how annoyed she is. Obviously, any parent might be delayed on occasion, but continual unexplained lateness is particularly annoying. Some private nurseries fine parents who are late, charging anything between £10 and £20 an hour or part of an hour. This is stated clearly on the admissions form and is part of the contract entered into by the parent.

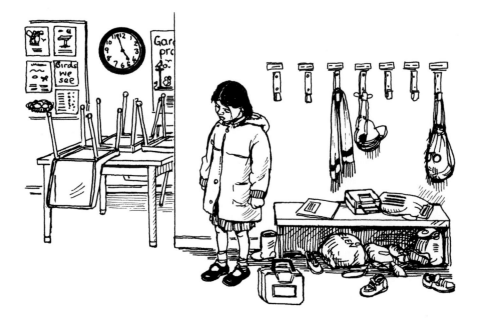

Some schools will appoint one of the staff to undertake liaison work with families. Part of the role will be to monitor attendance, working closely with class teachers and the Education Welfare Service.

EDUCATION WELFARE SERVICE

The Education Welfare Service's main role is to help schools improve attendance and reduce unauthorised absence and truancy. Education Welfare Officers work closely with schools, children and their parents and with other statutory and voluntary agencies.

Advice and assistance will be offered but, if the parents fail to co-operate, legal action may be taken.

Bowes Primary School

Statement for **Family Liaison Work**

Co-ordinator: Date:

This document replaces the previous statement dated:

Rationale

All families need to be included and involved in the education of their children to enable them to reach their potential and participate fully in school life.

- Monitoring attendance
- School admissions
- Liaise with families referred by teachers

Guidelines

Attendance

Ensure staff are clear on completion of registers.

Monitor registers regularly and contact parents where a child's absence is causing concern. A series of letters are sent home according to the stage of concern.

Follow up letters if no change has been seen and work with families to improve attendance.

Liaise with the Education Welfare Officer and refer families if necessary.

Admissions

Show new families around the school, helping with completion of forms, and introduce families to class teacher.

Explain school induction pack given to new families.

Follow up new admissions ensuring that children settle well and that parents are fully involved in their child's education.

Other work with families

Class teachers consult with the Special Educational Needs Co-ordinator, who then refers appropriate families to the co-ordinator using a referral form.

Addictive parents

Becoming addicted to anything can be damaging but some addictions are more damaging than others. For example, being addicted to daytime television does not necessarily cause harm to the family, although some might think that the time could be better spent. Being a gambler or a shopaholic can cause the family a great deal of financial hardship, and the parent needs help either to restrict or to stop the habit. But a hard drug or alcohol abuser will put his/her addiction in front of anything else, and may well resort to crime to obtain the money to continue the habit. These parents can be found in any stratum of society, although some may hide it better than others.

The impact on the family can include emotional, social and financial problems. Feeding a habit means less money to meet the needs of the children, and poverty can result. The parents are likely to spend less time with the children because the one with the addiction is monopolising the attention of the non-abusing parent. Socially, the children may feel unable to invite friends round to their home and reluctant to leave the parent alone for fear of what might happen.

ALCOHOL ABUSE

It has been estimated that 1,000,000 children in the UK are growing up in families where at least one parent is a problem drinker. According to

the National Society for the Prevention of Cruelty to Children (NSPCC), in 60% of fatal child abuse cases alcohol or drug abuse is involved. Alcohol contributes to 40% of domestic violence incidents and 25% of child abuse cases.

There are groups that exist to help the families of alcoholics, but it is sometimes difficult to get the alcoholic to recognise how serious the problem is becoming.

CASE STUDY

Joanie has two children in the school, Paul aged 6 and Louise aged 3 in the nursery class. The family is well known to social services.

One day Joanie arrives to collect Louise, staggering all over the place and smelling of drink. In front of the children and some of the parents she opens her coat to reveal that she has nothing on underneath.

When the staff remonstrate with her she yells, 'What do you expect me to do? I've no money and this is the only way I can earn some.'

1 What immediate response should the staff make?
2 How can the establishment help the children?
3 Can the school support Joanie more?
4 How can the school and social services work together?
5 What other agencies can be involved?

DRUG ABUSE

Parents who use unprescribed hard drugs are doing so illegally, but this may not be obvious to the establishment. Despite media attention, these parents are not necessarily uncaring and neglectful. Many parents who take drugs limit their use to specific times and places and are careful to ensure that the child is not present. Other parents, with a more erratic pattern of consumption, may not always be in control and the children may be at risk.

HOW THE ESTABLISHMENT STAFF MIGHT HELP

To help in any way, the parent must trust the staff to maintain strict rules of confidentiality, and have built up a good relationship in the first place. It may well be necessary to obtain the parent's permission to put them in touch with outside helping agencies.

All early years' staff are committed to putting children first: 'the welfare of the child is paramount' (Children Act 1989). If any member of staff feels that a child is endangered by a parent addicted to drugs or to alcohol, there is a duty to support the child, and child protection procedures may have to be initiated.

Abusive parents

It is very difficult to predict the circumstances in which abuse takes place; nevertheless, many researchers have suggested that there may be some predisposing factors in individuals. These may relate to the adult's personality and background, to problems in the adult's life and environment, and to factors relating to the child. Beaver *et al.* (*CACHE Level 3 Child Care and Education, 2008*) list the following factors as predisposing to child abuse.

- **Immaturity** – some people have not developed a mature level of self-control in their reactions to life and its problems. Faced with stressful situations, an adult may lack self-control and react strongly just as a young child might, in a temper or with aggression.
- **Low self-esteem** – some people have a very poor self-image; they have not experienced being valued and loved for themselves. If they are struggling to care for a child, they may feel inadequate and blame the child for making them feel worse about themselves because they are finding it difficult.
- **An unhappy childhood where they never learnt to trust others** – parents who have experienced unhappiness in childhood may be less likely to appreciate the happiness that children can bring to their lives. They have not had a good role model to create a happy and caring environment for their children.
- **Difficulty in experiencing pleasure** – an inability to enjoy life and have fun may be a sign of stress and anxiety. This person may also have problems in coping with the stress of parenting and gain little pleasure from it.
- **Having unsatisfactory relationships** – when parents are experiencing difficulties in relationships, whether sexual or other difficulties, this can form an underlying base of stress and unhappiness in their lives. There may also be a general background of neglect or family violence within which there is little respect for any individual.
- **Being prone to violence when frustrated** – the damaging effects of long-term family violence on children have been recognised. Research shows that children who regularly see their mother beaten can suffer as much as if they had been frequently hit themselves.

- **Being socially isolated** – parents who have no friends or family near-by have little or no support at times of need; they have no one to share their anxieties with, or to call on for practical help.
- **Adults whose responses are low on warmth and high on criticism** – in such families, children can easily feel unloved and negative incidents can build up into violence.
- **Having a fear of spoiling the child and a belief in the value of punishment** – some people have little understanding of the value of rewards in dealing with children's behaviour; they think that children should be punished to understand what is right; they think that responding to a child's needs will inevitably 'spoil' the child. They are more likely to leave a child to cry and not be warm and spontaneous in their reactions to them.
- **A belief in the value of strict discipline** – there are many variations in parenting styles, family structures and relationships; these are not necessarily better or worse than each other. They meet the needs of children in different ways. Some styles of discipline use punishment (both physical and emotional), rather than rewards. This is more likely however, to lead to abuse when other stressful factors are present.
- **An inability to control children** – parents under pressure seldom have much time for their children and are more apt to lash out in a rage at the frustrations of everyday interactions.
- **Not seeing children realistically** – this involves having little or no understanding of child development and the normal behaviour of children at different stages; such adults are more likely to react negatively to behaviour that causes them difficulty rather than accepting it as normal. They may punish a young child inappropriately for crying, wetting, having tantrums or making a mess.
- **Being unable to empathise with the needs of a child and to respond appropriately** – some people have difficulty in understanding the needs of children; they may react negatively when children make their needs known and demand attention.
- **Having been abused themselves as children** – these parents may have a number of unmet needs themselves and are therefore less likely to be able to meet the needs of a dependent child; they have also had a poor role model for parenting and family life.
- **Having experienced difficulties during pregnancy and/or birth, or separation from their child following birth** – research shows that difficulties during pregnancy and childbirth, or early separation of a mother from her child, can result in a parent being less positive towards a child. Faced with this child's demands, they may be less able to cope. They may lose their temper more quickly and resort to violence more easily.

All families behave differently, and some of the following factors might occur from time to time in families where there is no question of abuse. A number of these signs exhibited over a period of time, however, should cause concern:

- frequent smacking of and shouting at babies and children, often for behaviour that is developmentally normal, such as a toddler wetting her pants
- expecting the child to be the parent, giving love and comfort to the adult
- parental indifference to the whereabouts and safety of their children
- barking orders at a child, without displaying patience or clear explanations of what is expected
- never giving praise or encouragement
- unreal expectations of appropriate behaviour
- discouraging the child's natural curiosity and not providing enough stimulation
- seeing the normal behaviour and actions of a child as a deliberate act performed in order to upset and annoy the parent
- frequent rows and disagreements between the parents and other family members, perhaps leading to violence.

There are certain situations that parents find stressful. The NSPCC has identified seven stress behaviour situations that parents have to cope with:

- the child who will not stop crying
- defiance and disobedience
- children squabbling
- temper tantrums
- unfavourable comparisons with other parents by the child
- refusing to go to bed
- moodiness and argumentativeness.

By reacting to such situations with patience and empathy, you are showing a good example in how to deal calmly with challenging behaviour. Your appropriate response will have an impact on the child and the parent. The way you listen carefully to what both children and parents have to impart will show how much you respect and value their views and opinions. You will be able to advise families if they are going through stressful times, referring them to helplines like Parentline and the NSPCC, and finding out about local information for parents and carers. Most councils have leaflets especially written for parents, often in many different languages. You will reject violent responses to situations and show children and parents how to respond in an assertive fashion rather than resorting to aggression.

DOMESTIC VIOLENCE

Domestic violence features in over a quarter of reported violent crimes, but many incidents will remain unreported. The majority of violence is inflicted by the male partner on the female partner and, in a study carried out by the National Children's Home Action for Children in 1994, 83% of the men were father to one or more children in the home. Domestic violence is the second most common type of violent crime reported to the police and is found in all classes and cultures.

Violent men often threaten to harm their children as a way of controlling their partners. In 90% of incidents, children were in the same room or in one next door when violence took place.

The short-term effects of this violence on the children included:
■ problems at school
■ difficulty in making friends
■ emotional difficulties, such as withdrawal, aggression, displaying fear and anxiety.

The long-term effects included:
■ lack of self confidence
■ poor social skills
■ violent behaviour
■ depression
■ difficulties in forming relationships
■ disrupted education, resulting in failure to reach their potential.

Many mothers were frightened to reveal the extent of the violence to anyone, through guilt and from fear that the children would be taken away. One of the recommendations following this piece of research was that all children living in violent situations must be considered 'children in need' under the Children Act. A social worker should assess their needs in order to offer support, counselling and therapy.

Children who live within the shadow of domestic violence are often attacked and abused by the offender and without the example of a loving caregiver may go on to become abusers themselves.

WORKING WITH PARENTS WHO HAVE ABUSED

In this situation, one of the most useful things you can do is to show parents how to cope with the needs of children and their sometimes challenging behaviour. All children are lively, and challenging adults is part of their development. It is unrealistic to expect small children to be quiet and well-behaved day in, day out. Physical abuse is occasionally caused by parents under stress not being able to cope with what is really quite normal behaviour, particularly if they are depressed and isolated.

Encourage the parents to respond to challenging behaviour by:
- taking a deep breath and counting to ten
- remembering that they are mature and do not need to react like a child
- understanding and re-directing their anger, perhaps by punching a pillow
- remembering that young children can often be diverted by offering another activity
- going into another room for a short time, away from the child, collecting their thoughts and giving themselves time and space to evaluate the situation
- contacting someone on the telephone to express their feelings
- using local resources, such as drop-in centres and parent centres
- going outside, out of sight and hearing of the child, to scream and shout and let their feelings out
- trying to keep a sense of proportion.

If the person suspected of committing abuse is one of the child's parents, the other parent may need your support and advice, as s/he will be confused and upset about what has happened. The parent may need someone to talk to who will listen in a non-judgemental way, and may need information and help. This is very important to the child's eventual recovery and you will need to be as sensitive and supportive as possible.

You may be working with children whose abuse and neglect has been recognised while they are attending your establishment, or social services may request a placement for a child as part of a child protection plan. In some areas of the country there may be family centres where you may be working with the family together with other members of a multidisciplinary team, such as psychotherapists and social workers.

CASE STUDY

Andrew, aged 4½, is admitted to a family centre as part of a child protection plan. He has a much loved older brother, who is developmentally normal and attends the local Primary School. Andrew was rejected at birth and his mother often refuses to feed him or provide him with adequate care. He is short and thin and looks no more than 3 years old. His speech is delayed and his comprehension immature. His muscle tone is poor and he often falls down for no apparent reason. He spends a lot of the day alone in the book corner, rocking to and fro.

The centre team gives him three meals a day in the nursery – breakfast, dinner and a cooked tea. This does not help Andrew over the weekends. The mother is asked to attend the mealtimes and, although she is very reluctant at first, she is eventually persuaded to help prepare the meals and to sit with Andrew while he eats. This seems to break the cycle of neglect and she comes to accept Andrew as part of the family.

1 Why might some mothers neglect their children?
2 How would you involve Andrew's mother in helping to settle him into the nursery?
3 How might you help Andrew's mother prepare him for infant school?

Whatever the type of abuse, if you find yourself in the position of working with parents who have abused, you will attempt to:
■ acknowledge your feelings and seek opportunities to express them appropriately with colleagues and line managers
■ always remember that you need to work with the parents for the good of the child and therefore need to establish a working relationship
■ avoid colluding with the parents through fear of aggression

- talk and liaise with the other agencies concerned with the case, if required
- be aware of the child protection plan for this family
- record conversations and decisions taken with the family, using plain, jargon-free language
- request supervision of your work by a competent line manager
- acknowledge and relieve the stress of the whole family.

Remind yourself that when you are working with parents you are helping the child and playing a part in breaking the cycle of abuse. Try to assume a non-judgemental attitude and refrain from questioning the parents about the abuse, or from challenging information they may give you, as this is the task of other agencies. If the parents are coming to your establishment as part of a child protection plan, take time to introduce them to the unit and to the routines, giving them as much information as possible about the care of the child. Listen to what they are saying and express appropriate concern and kindness while remaining objective and empathetic.

You will need to foster the parents' self-respect and improve their self-image. It is hard for parents to understand where they have gone wrong, and they have to cope with the close scrutiny of their parenting practice by many different people, often finding it difficult to obtain a clear idea of what they are meant to achieve.

Although the task is challenging for the childcare practitioner, you will not be working in isolation and it is very worthwhile.

COPING WITH VIOLENT BEHAVIOUR FROM PARENTS

Violent behaviour does not happen very often towards staff in early years establishments, as there are fewer areas of conflict. However, almost any parent has the potential to react angrily, as the care and education of their children is an emotive issue.

The main causes of disagreement might be:

- the assessment and collection of fees
- admission policies
- management of challenging behaviour and resentment if their children are disciplined
- the assessment of children's educational needs
- attendance and punctuality
- disagreement over the needs of the children.

Some parents find it difficult to overcome the negative educational experience they endured. The parents themselves may be needy and under stress and the establishment has to understand and empathise with this. They might have negative feelings towards authority, and the staff have to work hard to make them feel valued and be careful not to be patronising.

If you feel threatened you should report the fact to your line manager immediately.

DO:

- remember your safety comes first
- report all incidents
- express your concerns and fears
- seek support if an incident occurs
- take someone with you if making a home visit
- refuse to accept verbal abuse.

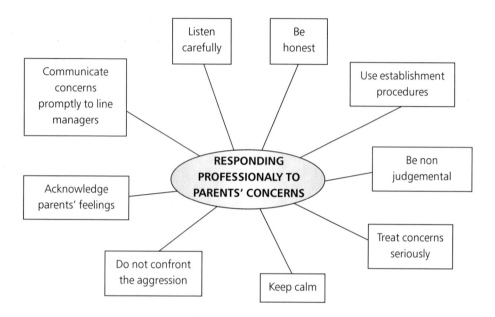

Activity

Watch your favourite 'soap' over the course of two weeks.

Look at a young child depicted in it. If you were a childcare practitioner looking after that child, what elements in that family might you be concerned about?

COPING WITH STRESS

Working with parents may cause a great deal of stress. Think about having:

- a discussion with your line manager – this may help you to examine your practice and look for alternative ways of working with the parents. It will be in both your and the parents' interests to help you sort out what is causing you stress
- an appointment with your general practitioner to discuss any symptoms you may have and to find out what sources of help are available

- personal counselling to help you reflect on your life style and to make possible changes
- courses on assertiveness, time management and relaxation techniques.

A knowledge of assertiveness skills will help you put your view clearly and purposefully.

Coping strategies:
- learn to say NO, and how to express your feelings and opinions
- look for support from and offer support to colleagues
- try not to take work home, and relax on your days off and on holidays
- manage your time more effectively, deciding what you want to achieve, the priority you give to each activity and the time and energy you are prepared to devote to it
- look after yourself by eating a healthy diet and taking regular exercise, and do not rely on nicotine, alcohol, caffeine or other drugs to keep you going
- relax in a hot bath or jacuzzi – saunas and steam baths also aid relaxation
- apply heat to the body using a heat pad or hot water bottle; this may reduce muscular tension
- try a massage, using aromatic oils
- explore complementary techniques, such as yoga and meditation, to reduce the effects of stress. They may also boost your ability to avoid becoming stressed
- develop new interests and hobbies
- talk about your feelings to others, and recognise your achievements
- be prepared to be flexible and do not live by rigid rules
- remember the good, positive things that have happened and do not focus on failures or difficulties.

Custody issues

The removal of a child or children by one parent without the consent of the other is an extremely distressing experience for the children and the parent that loses the child or children. The numbers of children involved in these cases appears to be growing, because of:
- cheaper and more accessible global travel
- free movement of people within the European Union and the reduction of border controls
- increased numbers of mixed marriages/relationships without a clear understanding of the cultural and religious customs of the other partner

- the fact that courts will now only make court orders defining residence if it is better for the child than making no order.

Parents who are married share parental responsibility for their children, including the decision as to where the child should live. The law does not require them to consult with one another in exercising their parental responsibility. Each may act alone. It is within the law for a married parent to remove a child from the home without the consent of the other parent, providing they do not remove the child out of the UK. Where there is disagreement between parents, an application can be made to the court for a residence order stating where the child should live, or possibly an injunction preventing one parent removing the child from the care of the other. The same circumstances apply on divorce, where no court order has been made.

When couples are in partnerships rather than marriage, the father only has parental responsibility if there is a parental responsibility agreement with the mother, a parental responsibility under Section 4 of the Children Act 1989 or a residence order. Unless any of the above circumstances exist, it is unlawful for an unmarried father to remove his child from the mother.

If you are working in an establishment, you need to be extremely careful only to hand the children in your care over to named and known carers with the authority of the parent. Never allow a child to go with someone about whom you are doubtful, however plausible they may appear.

If you are working in a private home, and one parent fears that the children may be abducted by the other, you should advise the parent to:

- encourage the other parent to remain part of the child's life, keeping in touch by letter and telephone, giving the parent regular information about the child's progress and development
- seek counselling and support services
- seek a court order containing a restriction against removal
- always make sure that the child/children are accompanied when away from home
- consult a solicitor with specific expertise
- keep the child's passport in a safe place, either in a bank or with a solicitor
- prevent the other parent from obtaining a birth certificate: this can be done by contacting St Catherine's House in London.
- arrange for contact visits to be supervised and do not allow the child to leave the country on a contact visit
- keep all important information concerning the children in a safe acces-

sible place, as quick action might be needed in an emergency. This information might include photographs of children and parents, copies of court orders, full details of the child's passport, telephone numbers of the police and solicitor, full details of the potential abductor.

All children born after October 1998 are required to have their own passport and not to share that of their parent.

The Hague and the European Conventions, ratified in August 1986, secured the return of children to their country of habitual residence, so that disputes can be resolved by the courts. There is no requirement under the Conventions that the welfare of the child is paramount, and the merits of the case are not examined. Where children are abducted to countries that are not subject to the Conventions, proceedings will have to be started in that country. This is a complex area and, if you should be involved in any aspect of it, you should advise parents to seek further legal advice.

Activity

Discuss within your group whether or not marriage between two people from different countries, with conflicting belief systems, is usually successful.

GOOD PRACTICE IN ENCOURAGING PARENTING SKILLS

1 Present yourself as a good role model in all areas of child care. Use a non-threatening approach at all times.
2 Build a trusting relationship with the parents, working with their strengths rather than their weaknesses.
3 Use praise and encouragement as positive reinforcement when the parent shows appropriate behaviour.
4 Work with the parents in planning the child's future care and development.
5 Listen to the parent and try to establish what particular areas of care they find most difficult.
6 Explain to the parents that some of the child's behaviour is quite normal for her stage of development.
7 Give help and information in dealing with any behaviour the parent finds difficult.
8 Discuss the importance of a consistent response and suggest appropriate and alternative ways of socialising the child.

Resources

Organisations

ChildLine, www.childline.org.uk
Cry-sis, www.cry-sis.org.uk
Kidscape, www.kidscape.org.uk
National Drugs Helpline. Telephone: 0800 776 6000
Newpin, www.newpin.org.uk
NSPCC, www.nspcc.org.uk
Women's Aid Federation, www.womensaid.org.uk

9 BARRIERS TO PARTNERSHIP WITH PARENTS

> **This chapter covers:**
> ■ **Barriers to communication**
> ■ **Developing strategies**

Working in partnership with parents is not always easy. There are many reasons for this: difficulties in communication, inexperienced staff, shortage of qualified staff, rapid turnover of staff, or a new head who does not yet know the local community. It is important to recognise where the partnership is not working as well as it might, and to look at how to improve relationships between the families and the establishment.

Barriers to communication

Occasionally, barriers appear that militate against working successfully and constructively in partnership with parents. Communicating positively is essential, but there may be barriers that prevent this. This could be because of factors within the establishment, such as:
■ physical access
■ security measures
■ limited time
■ use of jargon
■ too formal an atmosphere
■ staff lacking in confidence and experience
■ value judgements and assumptions on the part of the staff.
Sometimes the family finds it difficult to communicate with the establishment. This could be because of:
■ the family's lack of confidence
■ limited time
■ family conflicts
■ family literacy level
■ mental or physical illness
■ disability of a family member
■ lack of money
■ value judgements and assumptions on the part of the family.

FACTORS WITHIN THE ESTABLISHMENT

Physical barriers

Physical barriers prevent good communication. Some nursery schools are sited on the top floor of a block of flats or an office building, in some cases without access to a lift. This makes it very difficult for parents with smaller children to spend any relaxed time interacting with the staff, as they may be concerned that the pushchair will be stolen or preoccupied with how they are going to get down all those stairs again.

Lack of a room to talk privately to staff stops many parents from confiding in them about their problems at home or with their children. Some establishments have a special room for parents and this creates a very good atmosphere, where parents can get to know each other as well as the members of staff. Without this asset, the parents often feel in the way and do not wish to stay for any length of time.

CASE STUDY

Michael is the father of Lucy, aged 3, who attends a community day-care centre. One morning, when he brings Lucy to the centre, he is obviously very upset and Lucy is in tears. Tracey, Lucy's key worker, ▶

approaches them and asks them to tell her what is wrong. Michael bursts into tears, saying that his wife walked out the previous night after a terrible row. Other parents are listening. Tracey looks for a private place, but is unable to find anywhere.

1 Should Tracey have asked Michael what was wrong in front of other people?
2 Should establishments have a policy for dealing with upset parents?
3 How might Tracey be able to help Michael and Lucy?

Security measures

Many schools and nurseries now require parents and all visitors to be vetted in some way before entering the building. For example, parents may have to use an entry phone to gain admittance to a small cubicle where they sign a book before being let through another set of doors. This is to ensure the safety of the children but can be off-putting for parents.

There is tighter security today because of incidents at two schools in recent times, when a deranged person entered the premises and attacked staff and children. There is also fear of abductions, either by an estranged parent who does not have the right to take the child or by a paedophile. Faith schools often have very tight security because of the threat of terrorism.

In many schools, staff now collect children from the parents in the playground and deliver them back at the end of the day. Nurseries often have a member of staff at the door to check parents and children in and out of the building before locking the door during the course of the day.

Limited time

There are increasing demands on all members of staff, who have to write reports, record observations and undertake curriculum preparation. Home time can be chaotic and a difficult time for parents to talk with a member of staff. Appointments have to be made, which may mean the staff have to be flexible about their starting or leaving time. Problems that suddenly arise often cannot be dealt with immediately and may get worse while waiting for an appointment.

Use of jargon

Jargon is language used among professional people as a short cut to passing on information to each other. It is divisive if staff talk in jargon and

parents do not understand what is being said. For example, at a meeting designed to give some information to parents, if a member of staff constantly refers to the SENCO (the Special Educational Needs Co-ordinator) or NAI (non-accidental injury) without explanation, the parents might feel very left out.

A formal atmosphere
Many establishments have tried hard to break down the formal barriers that existed in the past, so as to make the parents feel more at home and not have to relive their own school experiences. A very formal and unwelcoming atmosphere can be intimidating to most parents. Efforts have been made to make the school environment friendlier and readily accessible.

> **Activity**
> List the advantages and disadvantages of children wearing school uniform.

Not all parents appreciate the less formal atmosphere and if it is carried too far it can look sloppy and unprofessional. A balance has to be achieved. For example, many staff are willing to be known to the parents by their first names, while still expecting the children to address them more formally. Staff need to find out how the parents would like to be addressed, without making assumptions.

There are often social gatherings of parents and teachers, some more formal, when information about the curriculum may be discussed, and some informal, such as quiz nights, discos and family clubs. There is a danger in some establishments of parents forming 'cliques' dominating the Parent–Teacher Association and all activities to do with parents.

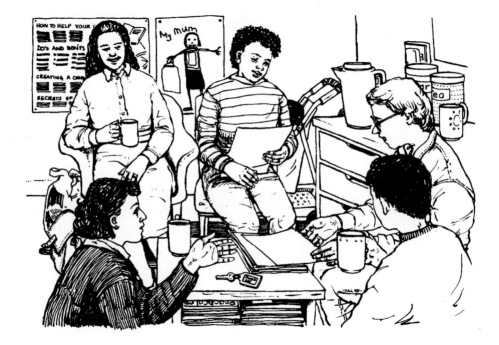

Lack of confidence and experience

Although it is now part of teacher training and the training of child-care and education practitioners to work in partnership with parents, it is often difficult when you are at college to gain much experience in this area, as you are so closely supervised. Newly qualified staff, therefore, often lack confidence and feel under scrutiny and exposed when attempting to establish positive relationships with parents. The rapid turnover of staff in some areas does nothing to assist in this. More experienced staff may feel that they have not been adequately trained to work with parents and that parents asking for advice and support across a range of issues might dilute their role as an educator. Some may be reluctant to share their professional expertise.

It is only by observing skilled practitioners that the newly qualified staff learn. It takes some time for the parents to trust new members of staff enough to confide in them. Staff need to be able to talk to their line manager about this aspect of their work.

If you are confident and have high self-esteem you will probably find it easy to build positive relationships. A person who does not feel good about herself may try to compensate for this by putting people down, erecting barriers and having a negative attitude.

Value judgements and assumptions on the part of the staff
Everybody makes assumptions about people. If you met a man after your car broke down you might assume that he could help you get it going – not always true! But by making these assumptions and judgements it is easier to use the knowledge you have about the human race and put it into pigeon holes. Some assumptions are unfair if they are based on prejudice and lack of information. For example, to assume that people belonging to a certain ethnic group are born with natural rhythm is patronising and incorrect. It would also be wrong to assume that all men with shaved heads belong to the British National Party.

Making assumptions about groups of people might mean that you fail to involve many parents in their children's education. You must constantly question why you think certain behaviour characterises certain groups.

FACTORS WITHIN THE FAMILY

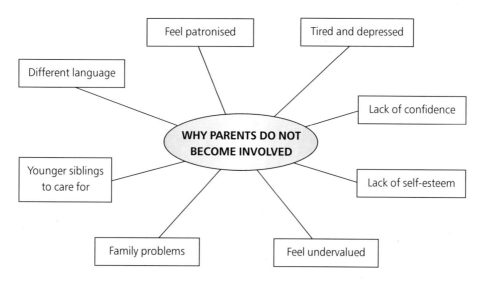

Lack of confidence

The parents may lack confidence in the school or nursery setting. This might be because of their own negative experiences of school or their attitude to anyone whom they perceive to be in authority. Some parents may not be conversant with the ethos of the school and yet be unable to voice their concerns or ask questions.

Time

There are many calls on the time parents are able to spend in the establishment. Many parents work; others might have a new baby or be involved in taking their other children to different schools or nurseries. Some parents might have dependent relatives living with them who need a great deal of attention. Other parents may employ an au pair, a childminder or a nanny to deliver and collect the children, trusting them to liaise with the establishment. Families who live at some distance might also find it harder to give time to becoming involved.

Family conflicts

Problems and conflicts within the family can be very depressing for the parents and make them unable to involve themselves fruitfully in educational projects. They may have to give time to seeing solicitors or counsellors. They may want to talk about their problems with the staff, or may forget to inform staff about changing family circumstances, such as custody issues.

Literacy levels of the family

It may be difficult for some families to take on board all the information the establishment might want to share with them, because of a low level of literacy or because English is not their first language. Many establishments try to address this by putting on classes, using interpreters or becoming involved in literacy programmes.

CASE STUDY

Colin teaches Year 1 and is keen to build good relationships with the parents of the children in his class. Leo, aged 5, has made an imaginative construction, and Colin would like his parents to see it and to discuss Leo's progress in general. In spite of repeated written requests, the parents have never been to the school, as the grandmother brings and collects him.

On asking the grandmother why he has had no reply to the notes he has addressed to the parents she tells him that neither her daughter nor her son-in-law understood the notes as they cannot read.

1 How could this situation have been avoided?
2 How can the school help the parents?
3 Who else might help the parents?
4 What support is there for Leo?

Mental and physical illness
Parents who suffer from an illness, either mental or physical, might not be able to liaise successfully with the establishment. It is possible that a member of staff, perhaps a key worker, might visit the child's home to keep up the contact. Working in partnership with this family might bring up issues of confidentiality.

Some parents can be angry and depressed, feeling powerless and experiencing low self-esteem.

Disability
Disabled parents might find access difficult. Hearing and visual impairments can be a barrier to good communication.

Value judgements and assumptions by the family
Parents who have not enjoyed or felt comfortable with their own educational experience do not realise how much attitudes have changed today and how much the establishment will value their input in their children's education.

Developing strategies

First impressions are important. Some establishments may not seem very welcoming at first because of the need for security and the safety of the children. Parents should be reassured that they are welcome to visit at any time, but will need to be conversant with the security procedures. Once these are explained, most parents will be glad that they are in place. To help parents feel comfortable in the establishment, a welcoming atmosphere and a friendly smile will go a long way towards making them more confident and therefore willing to participate in the life of the establishment.

Many schools and nurseries have a settling-in period for each child, and this is the time when the family can really get to know the establishment and the staff. The opportunity will be there to ask any questions and to observe the daily routines. The staff should encourage the parents to voice any concerns and give them some time during this period to make them feel at ease. Arrival and collection times are busy, but other times can be set aside to talk to parents. Late-afternoon and evening meetings can be arranged. Organising a crèche may encourage more parents to attend.

In some establishments, where practice has remained static, some parents may feel that their children's care and educational needs are not being fully met and may put forward a legitimate challenge. Staff should learn to listen, hear what the parents are saying and be prepared to look at their practice and make changes.

Practitioners need to understand the pressures that families face and learn to recognise parents' individual needs, so that they can be offered support, either long-term or short-term. Families experiencing unemployment or a low income may be offered sensible up-to-date advice and information on the monetary benefits available to them. Parents who are unwell or who are caring for dependent relatives may be informed about services that can offer support and advice.

Children's needs and parents' wishes may derive from a cultural or religious source, or have medical reasons, or quite simply, be what the parents want for their child. Parents' wishes and child-rearing practices must be respected and every effort must be made to comply with them.

There should be agreement and understanding about matters relating to:

■ food, its preparation and eating, and any special diet
■ personal hygiene
■ skin and hair care, for example creams and combs suitable for some African–Caribbean children
■ the question of clothing during play, for example, maintaining modesty in physical play, covering very curly or braided hair for sand play, or protecting against strong sunlight
■ periods of rest and sleep, for example routines and comfort objects.

Do not assume that, because a family is part of a particular cultural group, they follow all the practices of that culture. Some may observe all the customs of the group, while others pick and choose. To work in a positive way with all the families in the establishment, it is important to understand the variety of cultures with which you may be working, but the outward signs of a culture such as a way of dress, celebrating certain festivals and observing specific dietary laws is not the whole story.

Janet Gonzalez-Mena points out in her book *Multicultural Issues in Child-care* (1993) that there are five areas in which students need to learn communication skills. There are many cultural differences in the concepts of smiling, eye-contact, sensitivity to personal space, touch and time. Each cultural group also shares certain child-rearing patterns and has particular goals for their children. For example, many groups feel that it is cruel to follow the Western custom of making babies sleep on their own. Cultural groups are not immune to change, through education, more understanding of women's rights and the impact of the indigenous culture.

GOOD PRACTICE IN BREAKING DOWN BARRIERS

1 Respect all parents as individuals and learn from them different ways of child-rearing.
2 Contribute to a welcoming and relaxed atmosphere, encouraging parents to settle their children in and to spend time with them whenever they wish.
3 Avoid being patronising with parents. Listen carefully to what parents tell you about their children and remember that they are the experts on their own individual children.
4 Be professional at all times and never gossip about parents to other parents or within the team. If you should become aware of something that might affect the welfare of a child, go directly to your supervisor. Be careful not to jump to conclusions.
5 When working with parents from other cultures who do not have English as a first language, try to learn a few words of their language.
6 You may be involved in having to deal with an angry parent. Listen to what is being said, keep calm, and do not respond angrily yourself. Seek the help of your manager to sort out the situation.
7 Respect the rules of confidentiality, so that the parents will know they can trust you.
8 Be prepared to apologise if you are in the wrong.

Resource

Organisation

ParentLine, www.parentlineplus.org.uk

10 SHARING INFORMATION

> **This chapter covers:**
> ■ **Communication skills**
> ■ **Record keeping**
> ■ **Sharing observations**
> ■ **Emergencies**

In the past, many establishments were reluctant to share records and observations with parents, but this is now seen to be helpful for the children and is essential to establishing a positive partnership with the parents.

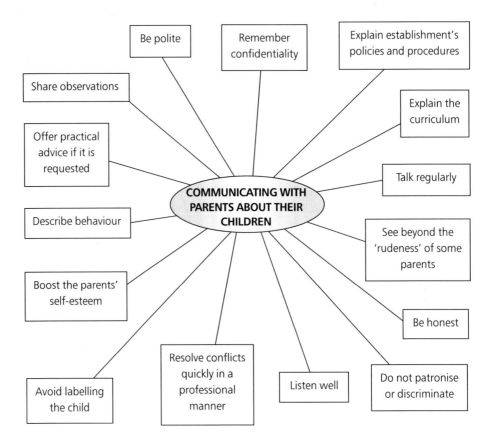

Sharing information helps the establishment and the parents to be consistent in many areas of child-care, such as behaviour, treating illness and encouraging educational attainment. There is an obligation for the establishment to keep the parents informed and up to date as to any changes. Most nurseries and schools will nowadays inform the parents in writing of:

- changes in staffing
- reports from the governors
- health and safety issues
- menus
- curriculum plans, long-term and short-term
- outings
- parent meetings
- infestations, such as head lice
- illnesses, such as rubella or chicken pox
- inset days
- changes in policies and procedures
- after-school activities.

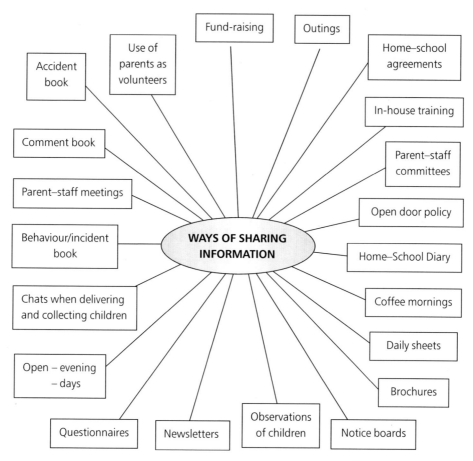

This information would either be posted on a parents' information board or in a letter to all the parents. Some establishments have a regular newsletter and many have websites. Establishments may distribute information leaflets about activities being held in the local community. Minutes of meetings of the Parent–Teacher Association are distributed regularly.

Some information may be given informally at parents' coffee mornings.

While some parents want to be fully informed of every aspect of the curriculum, the care and the routines, others, after an initial interview and close scrutiny of the last Ofsted report, will be happy to let the staff get on with it.

Communication skills

To disseminate information you need to have excellent communication skills, which include:

■ writing clearly
■ listening carefully

- speaking clearly and thoughtfully
- being aware of your body language
- assertiveness skills.

WRITING SKILLS

A professional person needs to be proficient in communicating information, ideas, directions and requests in writing and this will take many different forms. When writing for your own information, for example, a daily diary, a list of things to remember or a note to remind yourself to bring in certain objects for the home corner, you can record this information in whatever way is useful to you.

It will also be necessary to write:
- observations of the children
- a diary to share with the family
- reports concerning accidents or incidents
- taking and recording telephone messages.

Writing more formally
Any correspondence sent from the establishment must have the approval and permission of your line manager.

You may find yourself writing:
- a facsimile (fax)
- letters to individual parents
- circular letters to all parents, such as fund-raising letters
- leaflets
- reports to external organisations, such as social services
- assessment and recording of children's development to be passed on to the next school
- minutes of meetings
- agendas for meetings.

Whatever you are writing, remember to:
- be clear about the purpose of your correspondence
- use short sentences that convey your exact meaning
- check the spelling and the grammar
- keep a copy – use a black pen, as this photocopies well
- be as neat and legible as possible (the word processor is a great help)
- date all correspondence
- be professional, sticking to the facts and being objective
- avoid jargon and terms not necessarily understood by the recipient.

LISTENING SKILLS

It is as important to develop your listening skills as your oral skills. Being a 'good' listener does not come naturally to everyone. You need to listen carefully to parents, concentrate, look interested and not interrupt, and never finish sentences for other people. Ask questions if you need more information.

Remember that in some circumstances you may not be listening effectively. If you are worried or upset about something your concentration may be diverted. You may be distracted by other noises or movements in the room. Your feelings about the person may distort what you hear.

Listening is a positive activity, and therefore the good listener does not relax when listening but has to monitor and analyse what is being said in order to make an appropriate response. It may be necessary to indicate to parents that you are listening attentively by use of words such as 'Uhuh' and 'Mmm', which display interest and understanding. Sometimes, summarising what parents have just said (paraphrasing) is helpful, as it makes you listen carefully, lets them know if the message was communicated correctly and eliminates misunderstanding that might lead to conflict.

SPEECH

There is no better way of communicating than talking with people. This helps build relationships that using memos, notices, brochures and e-mails can never do. Always speak clearly, slowly and expressively, particularly when in formal situations or when the information you have to convey is particularly important. You will be using speech in informal day-to-day conversations with parents, colleagues and the children. From time to time you will be using speech to give information to parents and at other times using it in public discussion and debate, for example at parent evenings. Try to present one idea at a time and make sure that it is understood before continuing.

The drawback to using speech as a method of communication is that you have to make a quick response, which may be unconsidered and regretted later. Speech is generally not as precise as written language and it is unlikely that you will keep a copy or record. Be aware of the parent's background, knowledge and feelings, and what your ideas will mean to him/her.

Some parents may have difficulty in understanding written information, either because it is not in their home language or because they cannot read. With these parents, time must be taken to explain any necessary information face to face. Sometimes an interpreter is essential. Some people communicate better in speech than in writing, but for others it may be the other way round. You will need both skills to communicate effectively with parents.

CASE STUDY

Clara is head of an independent nursery school that caters for children in the local community aged 2–5. Nearly all the parents work and most children are brought to the school by nannies or au pairs.

Jessica, aged 3, has been in the nursery for two terms and seemed to settle in very happily. During the last 2 weeks she has started to bite the other children and their parents have complained. Clara has spoken to Jessica's au pair but, although she nods and smiles, her English is very poor and Clara is not sure that she has understood the situation.

1 Should Clara make direct contact with the parents?
2 What should Clara say to the parents of the children who have been bitten?
3 What information should Clara request from Jessica's parents?
4 How might Clara and Jessica's parents work together to resolve the problem?

BODY LANGUAGE

Remember that your body is sending out messages at the same time as you are talking and listening. All messages should be the same, but sometimes communication is spoilt when body language differs from what is being said. Think about:

- your posture
- eye contact
- facial expression
- energy level
- position of your feet and legs when sitting
- personal space
- touching others.

For example, while engaged in conversation with a parent, positive body language would involve maintaining eye contact, smiling, leaning towards the speaker and speaking at a moderate rate and in a reassuring tone. Negative body language would be yawning, looking or turning away, going off into a daydream and missing cues.

WORKSHOPS FOR PARENTS

You may have to address a group of parents, either in a workshop situation or in a larger meeting. At the start of any preparation, consider the purpose of your talk, what you wish to communicate and how you are going to present it. Remember to speak clearly, audibly and slowly enough so that the parents have time to take in what you are saying. Face your audience at all times, even if you are using visual aids. Try to eliminate distracting gestures; you might try practising in a mirror or before a friend so that you are aware of any irritating mannerisms.

Points to remember:

- be yourself and find your own style
- be positive
- accept that you will be nervous beforehand and try some relaxation techniques
- concentrate on the task, remembering that you are trying to communicate a message
- monitor your vocal expression, thinking about volume, pitch and speed and taking your time
- remember to articulate your words more clearly for a larger audience
- avoid too many statistics – put them in a handout to be distributed
- never apologise for your presentation

- if you forget your words, pause, take a breath, remember your objective and carry on.

ASSERTIVENESS SKILLS

Learning to be assertive allows you to be open in expressing your feelings and needs, and encourages you to stand up for your rights and the rights of others. It has nothing to do with aggression but is a technique that allows you to relate to others in an open and honest way, discussing problems and not personalities. Your assertive behaviour should encourage others to be assertive.

Being assertive will enable you to:
- handle conflict, dealing with difficult situations, where people are angry or upset
- be more confident, decisive and comfortable in your role
- communicate better, feeling able to express your view, identify problems and work together to find solutions
- reduce levels of stress
- develop professionally and personally.

Once you are clear about your expectations, they become easier to defend. Once you start to assert yourself, the approach is simple. You state your needs, rights and opinions in a clear way without qualification.

To develop your assertiveness skills you should:
- be natural. When asking for things, or giving instructions, do not apologise or justify yourself. Ask politely, and keep it short and to the point
- do not attempt to flatter or manipulate other people
- accept when other people say 'No', and do not take it personally
- if you say 'No', give a reason but do not apologise. Be calm and warm to show you are not angry or unhappy
- if you are interrupted, stay calm and continue to speak until you have finished.

Record keeping

The amount of paper work and administration has grown rapidly during the last few years, and a great deal of this is to do with keeping parents informed. All establishments are required by the Children Act 1989 to keep records of the name, address and date of birth of each child, the name, address and telephone number of the child's parents and records of attendance and punctuality.

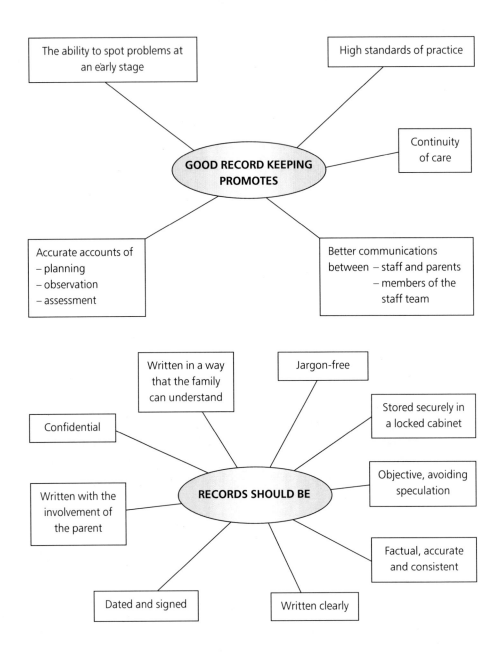

The ability to spot problems at an early stage

High standards of practice

GOOD RECORD KEEPING PROMOTES

Continuity of care

Accurate accounts of
– planning
– observation
– assessment

Better communications between – staff and parents
– members of the staff team

Written in a way that the family can understand

Jargon-free

Confidential

Stored securely in a locked cabinet

RECORDS SHOULD BE

Objective, avoiding speculation

Written with the involvement of the parent

Factual, accurate and consistent

Dated and signed

Written clearly

Settings delivering the Early Years Foundation Stage must meet the welfare requirements, which include a documentation section which makes it mandatory for providers to "maintain records, policies and procedures required for the safe and efficient management of the settings and to meet the needs of the children." (Also see pages 22 and 54). The records kept by settings will include:

- records of the child's progress
- consent forms, for example for going on outings or for accident and emergency treatment
- accidents and incidents
- the home language of the child
- any special needs, whether physical, dietary, social, educational or behavioural
- who is authorised to collect the child
- referrals made to other agencies
- child protection issues
- abusive behaviour from parents
- visitors to the establishment, so that everyone knows who is on the premises for security and health and safety reasons
- policies and procedures
- complaints.

Parents are entitled to access to their children's records. There may be exceptional circumstances, such as child protection issues, where parents may be denied access to the records, but this is rare. Establishments should inform parents about which records are kept and their purpose, where the records are kept, the format of the records and how and when parents can access them. Staff have to be objective in their assessments and records as these are now in the public domain.

All records should be held securely and only staff who need access to information should have it. Parents need to be assured that their privacy and confidentiality is maintained. When speaking to parents about a private matter, staff should make sure that this is done in a separate area, without anyone else being able to listen in.

If parents have a complaint about any incident or aspect of care in the establishment, it is important to deal with it quickly and a careful record should be kept of any action taken. All establishments must have a written complaints policy outlining the procedures to be followed.

An example of a record that might be kept by a nanny or a child-minder is shown on pages 158–9.

Care needs	
Child's name:	**Notes**
Toileting How often is the nappy changed? Where is it changed? What is used to clean the baby? How do you know when s/he needs to use the lavatory? Are there any unusual signals or words used? Is a nappy used at night?	
Food Does s/he have any allergies? Where does s/he eat? Is s/he given food choices? Is s/he expected to finish the meal? What happens if s/he refuses food? What table manners are expected?	
Dressing Who dresses him/her? Who chooses the clothes to be worn? Does s/he like privacy? Can s/he tie her own shoelaces?	
Separation How does s/he cope with separation? How is s/he distracted? How does s/he like to be comforted when distressed?	
Behaviour What is to be done when s/he is misbehaving? What is to be done when s/he is not co-operating?	

Care needs *continued*	Notes
Rituals Is there a special way of doing things at bath time, bedtime, rest time and mealtimes? Does s/he have a comfort object?	
Preferences Book Toy Food Drink Person Game Activity	
Friends Who is allowed to visit? Where do they play? Can s/he play at a friend's house, with or without prior permission?	
Domestic What chores is s/he expected to do?	
Activities Time on the computer Homework Watching TV Music practice Outside activities	
Medical concerns Past illnesses	

Bowes Primary School

Complaints Process – June 2008

> We want to ensure that all our pupils get the best out of their time in school. We want them to learn to participate in activities in school and to enjoy their education. If things go wrong, it is important that you get in touch with us immediately, especially if you wish to complain or express a concern.

If there is a problem you should speak first to:

The Class Teacher if the problem concerns:
- your child's work
- your child's general progress
- a behavioural issue concerning your child
- a disciplinary matter
- an end of year report.

If you are not satisfied with the outcome or consider the matter more serious please contact:

The Deputy/Assistant Head Teacher if the problem concerns:
- the curriculum
- your child's general progress
- the teaching of a member of staff
- a behavioural issue involving pupils or staff
- school arrangements or procedures

The Special Educational Needs Co-ordinator if the problem concerns:
- all matters relating to children with special needs.

> If you are still not satisfied with the outcome of the above, please contact the Head Teacher. If you are still not satisfied then please contact the Chair of Governors. The address is available through the school office. If you are unable to resolve your problem informally through this process you may register a formal complaint to the Governing Body.

Support and advice

Parents may wish to obtain advice at any of the stages. Advice is available from the Citizens Advice Bureau.

Through this procedure we aim to resolve all complaints quickly and amicably so that the needs of all our children are met.

REPORTS

Reports should be clear, honest and constructive and are at their best when they indicate what help the parents and the establishment together might give to the child. Individual factors need to be taken into account. A brilliant child who does well will obviously merit praise, but no more so than an average student who has put in a great deal of effort.

Reports should be kept up-to-date, presenting an ongoing record of achievement and progress, written in a way that does not encourage competition or comparison with other children. Concerns should be identified and recorded in a way that allows parents to discuss the issues constructively, while feeling supported by the establishment. Agreement should be reached as to appropriate action.

The curriculum and methods of assessment should be made clear to parents and every effort should be made to explain the terminology used. For example, it is pointless to put that 'she has reached Level 3' without an explanation of what that means. A parent who receives a report indicating a problem that has existed for some time would be understandably upset at not having been informed of this beforehand and not having some suggestions put forward as to how to help the child.

Activity
Discuss in your group how helpful you found your own school reports. Were they always accurate and constructive? Did you ever hide them from your parents?

Schools should give parents the opportunity to express their views of the child's progress; indeed many reports now provide space for the parents and the child to comment. All communication should be friendly and constructive. Regular information about the progress and achievements of the child is more helpful than just an annual report. In many schools now, computer programmes are assisting teachers to write regular reports.

Sharing observations

As you observe and record children's behaviour in your observations, you may well discover and identify information concerning the child and her family. Never record anything you would be unwilling to share with her parents. Because parents play the central role in their child's life, they should have the opportunity to provide information or correct any mistaken facts. You should never share information about the child with anyone without first seeking the parents' permission, unless you feel the child to be at risk of abuse.

When recording observations and making assessments, the parents are a vital resource as they:
■ know the child best
■ will understand why the child responds to activities and experiences in a certain way
■ will make a link to the home environment.

Some nurseries will take photographs of a child taking part in a variety of activities and present these to the parents in a book, allowing room for the child to comment on what is happening in the photos. The parents may add some home photographs to show some particular aspects of the child's home life, for example cuddling a new baby. Photographs of group events may be displayed in the nursery.

You will need to work with the parents when carrying out longitudinal studies, as there are obviously periods of time when the child is not in the establishment and you might want to know, for example, how the child spends the rest of the time at home, what her appetite is like and how well she sleeps.

If the child is going through a period when her behaviour is erratic, it is essential to discuss this with the parent as soon as possible, so that you might act together to help the child. Your approach to the parents should be sensitive to their feelings and any strategy devised to deal with challenging behaviour should be planned together with the parents and a review date set.

OBSERVATION AND ASSESSMENT IN THE EARLY YEARS FOUNDATION STAGE

Childcarers working in settings following the EYFS need to meet the standards for learning, development and care. Their responsibilities include:

- planning a range of play and learning experiences that promote all areas of learning
- assessing and monitoring individual children's progress through observational assessments
- using the findings of observational assessments to inform the planning of play and learning experiences
- ensuring that children's individual interests and abilities are promoted within the play and learning experiences.

ASSESSMENT REQUIREMENTS

Within the EYFS, ongoing assessment is an integral part of the learning and development process. The Department for Children, Schools and Families tells us that assessment should be underpinned by the following principles:

- Assessment must have a purpose.
- Observation of children participating in everyday activities is the most reliable way to build up an accurate picture of what children know, feel, are interested in and can do.
- Observation should be planned. However, practitioners should also be ready to capture spontaneous but important moments.
- Judgement of children's development and learning should be based on skills, knowledge, understanding and behaviour that they demonstrate consistently and independently.
- An effective assessment will take into account all aspects of a child's development and learning.
- Accurate assessment will also take into account contributions from a range of perspectives.
- Parents and other primary carers should be actively engaged in the assessment process.
- Children should be fully involved in their own assessment.

ASSESSMENT AT THE END OF THE EYFS

The EYFS profile is an assessment document. All registered early years providers are required to complete an EYFS profile for each child at the end of the academic year in which they reach the age of five. This provides year 1 teachers and parents with reliable information about each child's level of development as they reach the end of the EYFS. This enables the teacher to plan an appropriate curriculum that will meet all children's needs and support their continued development.

A practitioner will use their observations to make judgements and to record each child's development against the profile's 13 assessment scales. These are based on the early learning goals and divided between the six Areas of Learning and Development.

Activity
Visit the National Assessment Agency website at naa.org.uk/eyfsp to view the EYFS profile, the EYFS profile handbook, the Assessment Scales Guidance sheet and other support materials. You can also visit naa.org.uk/naa_19379.aspx to watch video clips that show children displaying behaviours that link with the assessment scales.

Emergencies

If there is an emergency at the establishment, parents need to be informed right away. Not all emergencies involve accidents. Evacuation of the premises should be practised at least once a term. Routes should be made clear and if parents are in the building they will be involved in leaving quickly.

All establishments will have policies and have accident and incident books to record emergencies. Each child will have an individual record form, completed by the parents, giving details of where the parents work, how they might be contacted and emergency contacts if the parents are unavailable. If a child has a special need, such as a susceptibility to succumb to anaphylactic shock if stung by a wasp, this should be noted on the individual record form and all members of staff should be made aware of it.

Medical/emergency information
Full names of children and dates of birth
Mother's name: Place of work: Telephone number: Mobile number:
Father's name: Place of work: Telephone number: Mobile number:
Family doctor: Address: Telephone number:
Contact if parents not available: Name: Address: Telephone number: Relationship:
Hospital of choice in an emergency: Address: Telephone number:
Health visitor: Address: Telephone number:
Children's allergies:
Children's medication:
Immunisation status:
Other essential information:

This page may be photocopied. © Oxford University Press 2009

CASE STUDY

The fire alarm goes off, and the teachers in the primary school collect their registers and promptly take the children into the far playground away from the school. The head teacher checks that everyone has left, only to find a parent in the Parent Room, drinking a cup of coffee. The Head politely asks him to evacuate the premises, but the parent refuses to go, as he has only just arrived, saying that it is only a practice for the children and he does not have to be involved.

1 What immediate action should the head teacher take?
2 How might this situation be avoided in future?

If a parent is unable to collect the child, an emergency person may be called upon, but this should be arranged with the establishment and a password should be agreed so that the staff are happy to hand the child over to someone they may never have met. This information should be updated regularly. If the child is not collected the Social Services Department will have to be contacted as they are in a position to find relatives who could take the child until contact is made with the parents.

GOOD PRACTICE IN SHARING INFORMATION WITH PARENTS

1 Spend some time, preferably each day, talking and listening to each parent.
2 Using a variety of different methods of media, make sure parents are kept fully informed.
3 Review and update records regularly.
4 Remember confidentiality!
5 Share observations of the child with the parent.
6 Write clear and relevant reports regularly.
7 Ensure that the parents are aware of emergency procedures.
8 Be an active listener and reassure parents that you are taking them seriously.

Working in partnership with parents is a key factor in good practice in working with young children. This applies not only to the head of the establishment but to all the staff, including the students. It needs all the people involved working together to provide a warm and welcoming atmosphere, where the parents will feel relaxed and confident that their children are being well cared for and stimulated to learn.

FURTHER READING

Campion, M. J., *Who's Fit to be a Parent?*, Routledge, 1995

Digman, C., *Working with Parents: A Guide for Education Professionals*, SAGE Ltd, 2008

Furedi, F., *Paranoid Parenting: Why Ignoring the Experts May Be Best for Your Child*, Continuum International Publishing Group Ltd., 2008

Hartley-Brewer, E., *Positive Parenting: Raising children with self-esteem*, Vermillion, 1998

Hobart, C. and Frankel, J., *A Practical Guide to Child Observation and Assessment*, 3rd Edition, Nelson Thornes, 2004

Roker, D. and Coleman, J., *Working with Parents of Young People: Research, Policy and Practice*, Jessica Kingsley Publishers, 2006

Skynner, R. and Cleese, J., *Families and How to Survive Them*, Vermilion, 1993

Whalley, M., *Working with Parents*, Hodder & Stoughton, 1997

Whalley, M. and the Pen Green Centre Team, *Involving Parents in their Children's Learning*, 2nd Edition, Paul Chapman Educational Publishing, 2007

Whalley, M. and the Pen Green Centre Team, *Working With Parents*, Hodder & Stoughton, 1997

INDEX

Page references in *italics* indicate illustrations and diagrams, those in **bold** indicate tables, charts or forms